FOUL DEEDS & SUSPICIOUS DEATHS IN PORTSMOUTH

Foul Deeds and Suspicious Deaths in
PORTSMOUTH

Sarah Quail

Wharncliffe Books

First published in Great Britain in 2008 by
Wharncliffe Books
an imprint of
Pen & Sword Books Ltd
47 Church Street
Barnsley
South Yorkshire
S70 2AS

ISBN: 978 184563 046 1

A CIP catalogue record for this book is available from
the British Library

Typeset in Plantin and ITC Benguiat by
Mousemat Design Limited

Printed and bound in Great Britain by CPI UK

Pen & Sword Books Ltd incorporates the imprints of
Pen & Sword Aviation, Pen & Sword Maritime,
Pen & Sword Military, Wharncliffe Local History,
Pen and Sword Select, Pen and Sword Military Classics
and Leo Cooper.

For a complete list of Pen & Sword titles please contact
PEN & SWORD BOOKS LIMITED
47 Church Street, Barnsley, South Yorkshire,
S70 2AS, England
E-mail: enquiries@pen-and-sword.co.uk
Website: www.pen-and-sword.co.uk

Contents

For former Inspector James Cramer
Historian of the Police of
Portsmouth

Preface

Three factors have shaped the history of Portsmouth - for good and ill. They are the sea, geography and war. The great natural harbour has provided a safe anchorage and ship-repair facilities, and the deep-water channel which hugs the coast of Portsea Island has brought ships safely to these shores on official business for almost a thousand years. Portsmouth's geographical position on the south coast, barely one hundred miles from the French coast, has also placed the town firmly on a natural line of communication between this country and continental Europe and, in due course, more faraway places. Thus, almost by default, Portsmouth has supplied this country for much of its history with what William Shakespeare described as the 'sinews of war': ships and men.

This role was recognised officially as early as the sixteenth century when the town was designated a royal dockyard and garrison town. What did all this mean for the people of the town? First and foremost it has meant that the history of Portsmouth is not just a local story, it is a regional, national and, often, an international story. This is reflected in many of the chapters in this book from the stories of Adam de Moleyns and Margaret Pole by way of George Byng and 'Jack the Painter' to the astonishing, and still topical, story of the life and death of Buster Crabb.

The town's naval and military history is therefore a thread which runs through almost all these chapters, not only those devoted exclusively to the naval and military but also those devoted to the 'ordinary' people of this town in the final section.

The last chapter is something of an exception to the rest of the book but I felt that it was worth celebrating the fact, little known outside the circle of Sherlock Holmes enthusiasts, that the most famous fictional detective in the world was born here, in Portsmouth, and that his first case was penned in a small room at the top of a house in Elm Grove, Southsea by a local doctor hoping to supplement his modest income as a general practitioner.

Acknowledgements

First and foremost, I must thank James Cramer, to whom this book is dedicated, for the help he gave me in the early stages of its preparation, and for so generously letting me use his files of newscuttings of articles he produced for the *Hampshire Telegraph* on law and order issues before that newspaper's untimely demise.

I should also like to thank the staff of the Local History and Naval Section in Portsmouth Central Library, and the Search Room team in Portsmouth City Museum and Records Office. I have met with nothing but unstinting assistance and advice on my visits. Both are priceless resources which we, the users, should cherish and support – and urge our politicians to do likewise. I am minded while on this subject of the words of the Reverend George Dawson (1821-76) in his inaugural address on the occasion of the opening of Birmingham Free Reference Library in 1866. The sentiments are equally applicable to our local museums and other artistic and cultural endeavours:

> *a Corporation Library...is the expression of a conviction...that a town like this exists for moral and intellectual purposes. It is a proclamation that a great community like this is not to be looked upon as a fortuitous concourse of human atoms or as a miserable knot of vipers struggling in a pot each aiming to get his head above the other in the fierce struggle of competition. It is a declaration that the Corporation of a great town like this has not done all its duty when it has put in action a set of ingenious contrivances for cleaning and lighting the streets, for breaking stones, for mending ways; and has not fulfilled its highest functions even when it has given the people of the town the best system of drainage – though that is not yet attained.*

I must also thank the Portsmouth City Museum and Records Office for permission to reproduce a number of the illustrations in this book. The provenance of these particular illustrations is acknowledged in the text. The rest of the illustrations come from the author's own collection or have been reproduced from either *Portsmouth in the Past* by W G Gates which was a limited edition of only 250 copies made up of topographical notes and sketches published originally in 1925 in the *Hampshire Telegraph,* or from W G Gates' *Records of the Corporation 1835-1927,* 1928, and *Records of the Corporation 1927-1930,* 1931.

Finally, I should like to thank my family – for their unstinting help particularly with technical matters.

Thank you, all of you.

Sarah Quail

STATE
MATTERS

CHAPTER 1

A Bishop is Removed
1450

J ust imagine the reaction today – locally, regionally, nationally and internationally – if the Prime Minister or a member of his cabinet was assassinated on the streets of Portsmouth! The news and known details of the crime would dominate radio and television bulletins as well as newspaper headlines, and the infamy and notoriety of the deed would be recalled long after the event and the prosecution of those suspected of perpetrating it.

Government House with the Garrison Church, formerly the Domus Dei, *behind. c. 1800* PMRS (Portsmouth Museums and Records Service)

Of course there were no news bulletins or screaming headlines in 1450 but some records do survive in monastic chronicles, and in the records of the bishops of Winchester, not only of what took place but what happened afterwards when on 9 January 1450 Adam Moleyns, bishop of Chichester, keeper of the privy seal, confessor and confidant of the king, Henry VI, was attacked and killed by a mob within or very near to the *Domus Dei* complex of buildings.

All that remains today of the *Domus Dei* is the Royal Garrison Church on the corner of Governor's Green, near the harbour mouth in Old Portsmouth. Anciently, it was one of a number of similar establishments built on the south coast in such places as Southampton, Arundel and Dover, and described variously as hospitals or hospices. They were not exclusively buildings established by the ecclesiastical authorities to care for the sick or poor. They were often places founded, generally in seaport towns, in the early medieval period to receive pilgrims on their way to famous shrines abroad, or strangers on business which was taking them overseas. Portsmouth was well-placed not only to receive travellers coming from the other side of the Channel to the great English medieval shrines at Winchester, Chichester and Canterbury, but also to serve as a staging-post, and as a gateway to places further south, for English pilgrims on their way to such places of devotion as St James's shrine at Santiago de Compostela in northern Spain, to Rome or even to Jerusalem itself.

Portsmouth was also a convenient port not only for soldiers and sailors but for diplomats on their way to English territories in France which may have been a strong consideration of the founder, Peter des Roches, bishop of Winchester, when he endowed the *Domus Dei c.* 1212 and equally, the reason why Adam Moleyns was seized there by a mob in the hospital grounds. According to surviving contemporary accounts the bishop was in Portsmouth 'for to make paiement of money to certayne soudiers and shipmenne for thair wages'. What happened exactly is difficult to disentangle but he seems to have been waylaid by a crowd of sailors and soldiers who had taken umbrage at official efforts to curtail their wages. '...it happid', said an anonymous writer, 'that with boiste[rous] langage, and also for abriggyng of thair wages, he fil in variaunce with thaym, and they fil on him and cruelly there kilde him'. He seems to have been seized at night within the hospital confines, perhaps while he was worshipping at the altar, dragged from the church

*The ancient dominions of the kings of England in France,
late eighteenth century engraving.* Caen Municipal Library

and through the churchyard towards the beach where he was murdered. This is the official version of events – that the bishop was killed by an enraged mob of malcontents. Today, however, it is generally accepted that, far from being a drunken brawl which ended in tragedy, this was a well-planned political assassination.

These were troubled times. The king and his advisers, led by William de la Pole, duke of Suffolk – the government of the day - were seriously discredited. English power in France had ebbed away with a series of humiliating military reverses and, without adequate naval forces in the Channel, piracy was rife and vital trade seriously disrupted. Parliament refused to do anything to alleviate the financial crisis which was exacerbated by official incompetence and corruption. By 1449 law and order had broken down and, as far as the public were concerned, the king and his advisers, led by Suffolk, and including Adam Moleyns, were to blame entirely for this hopeless state of affairs.

Who was Adam Moleyns? We do not know a great deal about his early life. He may have been the second son of Sir Richard Molyneaux of Sefton in Lancashire but we do not know for sure. His career prospered however due to his legal and diplomatic skills, and he was richly rewarded for his work.

He must have had friends in high places from an early age as he was presented by the crown to his first living – the rectory of Winterbourne Earls, near Salisbury – shortly before he was even ordained in 1423. Altogether he amassed during his lifetime some fourteen rectories, eleven cathedral benefices, two deanships (St Buryan in 1438 and Salisbury in 1441) and two archdeaconries (Salisbury in 1439 and Taunton in 1441) becoming, finally, bishop of Chichester in 1445. In extenuation, he held some of these positions only briefly but his reputation went before him as an infamous pluralist.

He was trained at Oxford, receiving his degree of bachelor of civil laws in 1430 and his doctorate in 1435. It was in that year that he undertook his first diplomatic mission to Rome, representing the government of Henry VI in the vexed question of the succession to the see of Worcester. He was commended afterwards by the pope, Eugenius IV, for his skills as an advocate. Further missions to Rome and to the court of the emperor brought rich rewards from king and pope. He took formal greetings from the king to other heads of state, and he dealt with the finer points of political alignments and peace treaties. Issues discussed with Pope Eugenius in 1442 included more domestic issues: the proposed canonizations of King Alfred and of Osmund, bishop of Salisbury in the late eleventh century, and requests from the king for indulgences for his new foundation of Eton College.

His association with Suffolk began probably in the late 1430s. He may even have become clerk of the royal council as early as 1436, although he was not appointed formally until 1438. He held this office until 1443. In the meantime, he was appointed second in command of the privy seal office in 1441, becoming keeper the following year. When he ceased to be the clerk in 1443 he became a full member of the royal council, and attended meetings diligently thereafter insofar as his diplomatic activities allowed.

He was employed almost full-time now on government business in France. He was the intermediary between the council and John Beaufort, duke of Somerset during the latter's preparations for his ill-fated French campaign of 1443. The following year he went with Suffolk to France to try and secure a lasting peace. This did not prove possible. A two-year truce was negotiated however, and the marriage of the king with Margaret of Anjou. He was also among the delegation which greeted a French embassy in England in the following year, and accompanied them on their return to France in the hope that somehow a settlement might be secured. He also played a key role in the highly unpopular negotiations to do with the cession of the county of Maine to the French between 1445 and 1448, and the fruitless efforts to secure a peace which would hold but which culminated finally in the resumption of hostilities in the summer of 1449.

Fatally, as it turned out, Adam Moleyns got involved in a dispute at this time with Richard, duke of York over his, York's, behaviour as the king's lieutenant in France. York accused the bishop of circulating rumours about financial irregularities and incompetence in the management of the security of Normandy. Moleyns denied responsibility for the rumours but did not deny that they were in circulation. In due course York was replaced.

Rouen, the Norman ducal capital, fell to the French in October 1449. English public opinion was outraged. The brunt of the anger was directed at Suffolk but Moleyns' long association with government policy in France left him exposed to the criticism as well. He clearly took stock of his affairs and decided that now was the time to retire from public life. He obtained a royal licence in December to resign from his secular offices and to go on a pilgrimage. His excuse was failing health and a guilty conscience from neglect of his diocesan duties. And this was why Adam Moleyns, bishop of Chichester, was in Portsmouth early in the new year of 1450. He was waiting for a suitable boat or possibly better weather to make the crossing to France, as he had doubtless done on many previous occasions. It is curious therefore that a number of sources say that he was in Portsmouth on government business - to pay the troops in the town waiting themselves for passage to France. Would this really have been appropriate business for such a prominent individual: a bishop, a member of the King's Council and a diplomat?

Might this not have been a subterfuge for what really happened – that he was in fact murdered deliberately by someone who bore him a more personal grudge? There were doubtless a number of people who nursed grievances but none more so than Richard, duke of York, retired ignominiously for reasons which Moleyns had not chosen to deny – and the Yorkists were now in the ascendant.

One Cuthbert Colville has been cited as the man who struck the blow which fatally felled the bishop. If this was indeed the case, it certainly lends credence to the theory that York conspired to do away with Moleyns, as Colville was at one time in his service. It would not have been difficult for a professional assassin to disguise his activities. Portsmouth had experienced more than its fair share of the problems besetting the country at this time. Successive expeditionary forces had mustered here in recent years and another such force was assembling in Portsmouth in late 1449. By the end of the year there were nearly 5,000 men encamped on open ground to the north and east of the town and its few hundred residents. Poorly led and their wages long overdue, they were becoming increasingly disaffected. It was an ideal recruiting ground for an *agent provocateur.* Certainly by the next century it was believed to be a political assassination. John Stowe repeated the story that Moleyns had been slain 'by shipmen' but believed that the deed had been done 'through the procurement' of York.

Interestingly, no accounts suggest that local men were involved at all but at the time it was the town of Portsmouth and its people who were held responsible by the church for the crime and who paid the price: 'the sentence of Greater Excommunication', a sentence which was not lifted until 1508, almost sixty years after the crime was committed.

In theory this sentence meant that the people of the town were cut off from participation in the sacrament and all communication with the church. The baptism of infants, confessions of the dying, marriages, burials in consecrated ground, the celebration of mass and other religious feasts and ceremonies were all forbidden, and the bells of St Thomas's should have fallen silent.

What the sentence meant in practice is not easy to establish. It is significant that the parish church does not possess a Norman font, smashed symbolically perhaps in 1450 to prevent baptisms. Sixty years is a long time however for a town to be deprived entirely of the comforts of the church and scholars believe today that as long as the vicar and his congregation behaved discreetly, a *status quo* of sorts was tolerated by the diocesan authorities. Eric Kemp, the ecclesiastical historian and a more recent bishop of Chichester, wrote to Portsmouth historian John Webb several years ago that

> *there was almost always in the Middle Ages a good deal of difference between theory and practice and it is never very safe to assume that what was laid down in theory in the Canon Law was in fact what happened in detail.*

In fact John Webb has calculated that at least sixteen vicars were appointed between 1450 and 1508.

It is also questionable whether the town was as badly affected socially and economically during the period of excommunication as vicar and parish insisted it was some sixty years later during the process of reconciliation in 1508. They claimed then that plagues, flood, fire and dearth had destroyed the town: 'by pestilences and other weaknesses more of the inhabitants there for the greater part were dead', 'and their land was not fertile but rendered sterile'; 'merchants, on account of the said crime and by reason of the infamy of such inhabitants, have been unwilling to call at the port there with their ships', and besides this, 'their lands in the various places had been inundated and devastated by the water, and the inhabitants there had sustained very many other damages and losses through water'.

The litany of woes continued: 'the buildings of that town and of other neighbouring places had been often consumed by fire' and finally, that harvests universally had been poor and more particularly 'the grass in the place where the said Bishop suffered, with the land on each side, is withered and does not flourish; and thus their habitations were deserted, insomuch that they could scarcely find any persons who wished to inhabit them, and so their buildings have fallen to ruin, and the inhabitants there have been marked with perpetual infamy'.

Original sources are limited but what little evidence there is would seem to indicate that conditions were not really as bad as the process would have the reader believe. The wool and wine trades still carried on, Portsmouth was a safe haven for local men engaged in piracy in the English Channel who brought their booty into Portsmouth to sell and, by the 1480s, royal officials, merchants and other travellers were passing regularly through the port without hindrance of any sort. More importantly, in the 1490s the king himself, Henry VII, decided to develop Portsmouth as a naval base. It was clearly time now to draw a veil over past events.

To atone for the alleged crime, the people of Portsmouth had first to be reconciled to the church in an elaborate process which was supervised by commissioners appointed by the bishop of Winchester and led by the abbot of Titchfield and the prior of Southwick.

At 7.00 am on 6 April 1508 the people of Portsmouth, led by their vicar, Robert Adam, met at the parish church. They were directed from there to the Domus Dei where they were met by the bishop's representatives who refused them entry, driving them away in fact with rods. Retreating to the site of the murder itself nearby, they were greeted by one Brother Hugh, an Observant friar from Southampton, who advised them to make their way back now to the parish church with their feet and legs

Early nineteenth century artist's impression of the medieval St Thomas's Church. PMRS

bared and there, prostrate themselves outside the west doors in prayer, and ask for penance and absolution. This they did. They were then charged again – to return once more to the Domus Dei and, prostrating themselves anew, recite the Lord's Prayer fifteen times and the Apostles' Creed three times while the commissioners repeated the seven penitential psalms and further chastised them. They returned finally to the parish church where they were absolved at long last of the crime which it is unlikely they even committed and with lighted candles in their hands, they were readmitted to the church.

The town was also required to erect a cross on the site where the bishop was felled, and as soon as possible thereafter to build an expiatory chapel where, thereafter, on Good Friday, the people were charged to go and pray for the soul of the bishop and all the faithful departed, and make an offering, presumably of cash, according to their means. Further, within three years, as many people as possible should travel to his grave and seek forgiveness in the name of all the inhabitants, and on 9 January each year, the anniversary of the murder, one at least from each family should go to the chapel and take part in a requiem mass for the repose of the bishop's soul.

The chapel was built promptly. It is shown on sixteenth century maps of the town between the Domus Dei and the sea wall. Nothing survives. It ceased to be used as a chapel during the turbulent years of the English Reformation when such chapels were dissolved, probably in the early 1540s. It was described in an inventory of buildings in 1565 as 'a certain small house formerly a chapel situate upon a green near the platforme'.

Adam de Moleyns was probably buried in Chichester, in his own cathedral church. His tomb is unmarked and its whereabouts unknown today, desecrated perhaps in the spoilation which took place when Parliamentary troops rampaged through the building in December 1642.

CHAPTER 2

The Countess is Attainted for Treason

1537

There is a well-known print of Warblington Castle which was published in 1785. The castle is essentially a ruin. There is a tall octagonal turret, and the remains of a gateway. An eighteenth century gentleman, with his dog at his side, rests on his stick in the bottom right-hand corner of the picture, contemplating the general landscape. Trees frame the view. It is an idyllic scene but one which belies the turbulent events which unfolded there

Warblington Castle, Hants, 1785 Author's collection.

during the dynastic and religious upheavals of the early sixteenth century when Warblington Castle was the home of noblewoman Margaret Pole, a member of the royal family.

Cousin of Henry VIII, she was countess of Salisbury in her own right from 1512 and in her younger days a possible Yorkist claimant to the throne itself. Born Margaret Plantagenent in 1473, she was the daughter of a younger brother of Edward IV, George, duke of Clarence, and his wife, Isabel Neville, eldest daughter and co-heir of Richard Neville, earl of Warwick and Salisbury, known as the 'kingmaker' for his role in deposing Edward IV in 1470 and restoring the puppet Henry VI.

Margaret was attainted of treason in 1537, imprisoned in the Tower of London and executed there on the orders of her kinsman, the king, Henry VIII, in 1541. At the time of her death, she was the last surviving member of the Plantagenet family which had ruled England since the twelfth century.

The manor of Warblington had come into Margaret's family in 1349 when it was inherited by another Margaret, the wife of Sir John Montagu. Sir John died in 1394–5 and the manor came down through his family, often through the female line, to Margaret Pole's mother, Isabel and, in due course, to Margaret's brother, Edward, earl of Warwick, who became the chief Yorkist claimant to the throne after the death of Richard III at Bosworth in 1485. He was executed for treason however in 1499 and his lands, including the manor of Warblington, were confiscated. They were restored to his sister – and heir – in 1512 with the earldom of Salisbury. As countess of Salisbury she was the only woman in England in the sixteenth century, with the exception of Anne Boleyn, who was a peer in her own right. She held lands in some seventeen counties, chiefly in the Midlands and the south of England but also in Wales and in Calais. Her income from these properties made her one of the wealthiest peers in the land. Her principal residence was Warblington Castle which she commissioned in 1517 when she must have believed that at last the trials and tribulations of her earlier life were at long last finally over.

Warblington Castle was clearly a fine building. The ruins depicted in the eighteenth century print still exist. The tall octagonal turret can be glimpsed through trees from the nearby motorway, and gives some idea of the castle's original scale. It is of red brick and stone and enough survives to show that the building must have been of four stories with square-headed, mullioned windows with arched heads to the lights. A survey of the property was undertaken in 1632 for a later owner, Richard Cotton, but it is essentially a description of Margaret Pole's house.

The use of the word 'castle' is something of a misnomer. Warblington Castle was never a significant piece of defensive architecture like the castles built by Henry VIII at Calshot, Hurst, Netley or Southsea to protect Hampshire's coast against the French. It was in fact a large moated early Tudor manor house. It was constructed of brick and stone and was of great 'receipt' which means that it was large, and indeed the surveyor went on to state that it was 'built square in length 200 foot and in breadth 200 foot'

> *with a fare grene court within and buildings round the said court with a fare gallery and divers chambers of great room and two towers covered with lead with a very great and spacious hall parlour and great chamber And all other houses of offices whatsoever necessary for such a house with a very fare chapel within the said house and the place covered all with slates and stones.*

Adjoining the house and covering some ten acres altogether was also a 'a fair green court' before the gates, a 'spacious' garden with pleasant walks, a grove of trees, two orchards and two small meadows. There was also 'a fare fishe pond' nearby and two barns, one of six bays and the other of four bays, with stabling and 'other out houses'.

The house was built on the high point nearest to Warblington Creek, probably on the site of the original Saxon hall and its medieval successors. The adjacent land seems to have been emparked in the fifteenth century according to manorial records. The creek is only a shallow depression today, occupied by a stream flowing down its old eastern side to the top of nearby Chichester harbour. However, before the upper reaches of the harbour began silting up and a containing wall was constructed across the mouth of the creek, probably in the late seventeenth century, there was possibly a navigable waterway reaching almost to the manor house itself. There was certainly sufficient water to supply Warblington mill which stood where the original main street of the village, leading from Church Lane by the side of the castle westwards towards the creek, crossed the stream.

Warblington Castle was described in a letter written during

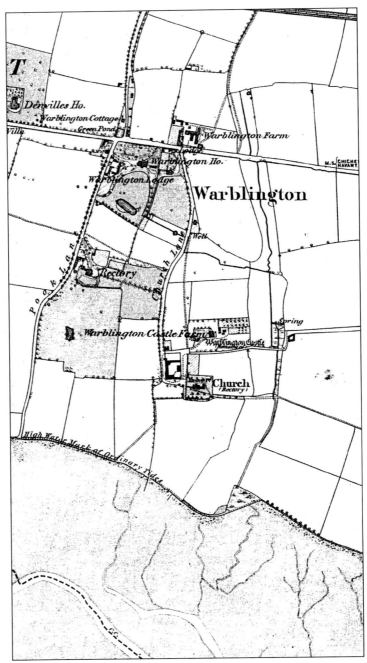

Warblington, from the 1860 Six Inches to One Statute Mile O.S. Map. PMRS

the Civil war in 1643–4, shortly after it had been besieged and captured, as 'the strong house at Warblington'. Clearly there was still a useful navigable channel nearby as according to the writer it commanded 'a pretty port' which would be of 'good advantage' to his side.

Margaret Plantagenet survived the dynastic upheavals of her childhood against the odds. Henry VII's claim to the throne was not strong and if he was to consolidate his hold on the kingdom he had to deal with those Yorkists whose claims to the throne were more valid than his own, beginning with the five daughters of Edward IV, and Edward's nephews, Clarence's son, Edward, earl of Warwick, and his sister, Elizabeth's, son, John, earl of Lincoln.

It is no exaggeration to say that Henry set about systematically eliminating the risks these people posed. He married Edward IV's eldest daughter, Elizabeth of York, himself, and found suitable husbands for three of the other princesses. The fourth, Bridget, chose to enter a convent. As for the men, Lincoln fell at the battle of Stoke on 16 June 1487 which was the culmination of the Lambert Simnel uprising which championed the cause of Edward, earl of Warwick, Margaret's brother. Warwick himself survived this particular upheaval. He was, after all, a prisoner in the Tower throughout – Henry had shut him away there early in the reign – but it was his misfortune that his name was used repeatedly by parties bent on overthrowing Henry, and when he attempted to escape from the Tower in 1498 with Perkin Warbeck, at the same time as yet another attempt to impersonate him, Henry decided, reluctantly, that Warwick had to go. He was executed for treason in 1499.

Lincoln's brothers, the de la Poles, and their cousin, William Courtney, attempted, unsuccessfully, to foment further rebellion in the new century. Edmund de la Pole, earl of Suffolk, fled abroad with his brother Richard in 1501, and attempted to rally support for the Yorkist cause but succeeded only in ensuring that his brother William and cousin Courtney, and their supporters who were still in England, were rounded up and sent to the Tower, some to their deaths.

Suffolk himself was handed over by the Burgundians to Henry some five years later and sent to the Tower himself. Richard made his way to the French court where he was actually recognized in due course as the King of England but this only sealed Suffolk's fate. He was executed in 1513. Finally, in 1525, Richard himself fell at the French king's side at the battle of Pavia.

Like her cousins, the Princesses of York, Margaret had a marriage arranged for her by Henry who hoped that she would be unlikely now to become a figurehead herself for any Yorkist plots. She married Sir Richard Pole shortly after the battle of Stoke in 1487. Sir Richard was a Welshman. He was in fact a kinsman of the king and became in due course one of his most loyal and trusted servants, serving him in many different capacities over the years – as an esquire of the body and as constable of a number of the Welsh castles, as sheriff of Merioneth and as chamberlain of north Wales and chamberlain of Chester. He was also a member of the council of Wales and the marches, justice of north Wales and lord chamberlain to the king's eldest son, Prince Arthur, when the prince's household was established at Ludlow in 1493. He also assisted at the proxy wedding of Prince Arthur to Katherine of Aragon in 1499. In the same year he was elected to the Order of the Garter.

Although Margaret's marriage was an arranged one, it seems to have been happy. Sir Richard is described by one writer as being capable, loyal and with an endearing personality. For the first time in her life, Margaret may well have felt that she had found some stability. Her own childhood had not been easy in the fierce civil wars of the late fifteenth century. Her mother died in childbirth in 1476 when she was three, and her father, Clarence, was arrested and confined in the Tower for treasonably plotting against his brother, the king. He died there, drowned, probably murdered, in a barrel of malmsey in 1478.

The two orphans, Margaret and her brother, Edward, earl of Warwick, were raised at the royal palace of Sheen with their uncle's, Edward IV's, children and when Edward himself died in 1483 they went to the court of the new king, Richard III, another uncle. There, on the death of Richard's son, Edward, Prince of Wales, Edward of Warwick became briefly the heir to the throne, and Margaret was given the title of Princess Royal before John, earl of Lincoln superseded her brother as Richard's heir.

After Bosworth brother and sister were separated. Whether they ever saw each other again is unknown. Edward was sent to the Tower, his claim to the throne through the direct male line posing too great a threat to the new king, Henry VII. A husband was identified for Margaret.

Margaret bore Sir Richard Pole five surviving children: Ursula, Henry, Arthur, Reginald and Geoffrey. Henry and Arthur, the two eldest boys, were clearly named after the family's royal patrons. Margaret and the children seem to have followed Sir Richard as he undertook his official duties, settling where possible nearby. Margaret herself became a member of Katherine of Aragon's household in December 1501, and so began a friendship with the young Spanish princess which lasted for the remainder of Katherine's life, although Margaret left Katherine's service after Prince Arthur's death in 1502. Sir Richard continued to be employed however on royal business, accompanying Princess Margaret to Scotland in 1503 for her marriage to King James IV. Sir Richard died though in 1504. His widow was thirty-one. She had five young children and few financial resources.

Her fortunes improved however when Henry VIII came to the throne in 1509. He almost seemed anxious to make amends for the injustice done to her brother Edward. She was granted an annuity of a hundred pounds immediately, and shortly after Henry married his brother's widow, Katherine, in 1510 – a union which had been determined by his father, Henry VII, who had been anxious to lose neither the girl's dowry nor the Spanish alliance - Margaret became one of the ladies of the new queen's chamber. Finally, she was restored to the earldom of Salisbury and all the lands her brother held at the time of his death, and the barony of Montagu was revived and conferred on her eldest son, Henry, who carried out on her behalf those duties of a great magnate which her sex – and the times – precluded her from executing such as sitting in the House of Lords, representing her on commissions of the peace and leading her troops into battle.

Her third son, Reginald, also enjoyed the king's favour. Destined for the church from an early age, he was educated at the Charterhouse at Sheen and then by the Carmelites at Oxford before going on to Magdalen College, Oxford. When he left Oxford, the king himself paid for Reginald to study abroad. He went first to Padua at Henry's expense in 1521, returning to England in 1527, and two years later, in 1529, the king paid for him to study in Paris. As for her other children, her second son, Arthur, made a career for himself at court. Her daughter, Ursula, as a member of the royal family, was considered as a possible bride for the duke of Milan in 1516 but in 1518 she made a spectacular marriage with Henry Stafford, the son and heir of the duke of Buckingham.

Margaret was a cultivated and devout woman, described by the king himself in happier times as 'the holiest woman in his kingdom'. She supported the 'new learning', the rediscovery of the language, literature, and antiquities of Greece and Rome, and was a patron of humanist scholars. She was a loyal friend and ally of Katherine's throughout the queen's life. At the baptism and confirmation of the Princess Mary in 1516 she was confirmation sponsor and in due course, some years later, governess and head of the household at Ludlow where the princess lived for a time. The princess held her in great affection and there was even talk of Reginald being chosen by Katherine as a possible husband for her daughter.

When Katherine was banished and subjected to the indignities and humiliation of the royal divorce, Margaret supported the queen and her daughter steadfastly. Her famous refusal to surrender the princess's jewels and plate for the use of Anne Boleyn in 1533 led to her dismissal as the princess's governess. Other issues contributed to her deteriorating relationship with the king. There were suggestions that she was involved in the affair of the outspoken young visionary, Elizabeth Barton, the so-called 'Nun of Kent' who seems to have been used as a tool by those opposed to the divorce, and there were wrangles with Thomas Cromwell over the appointment of the prior of Bisham Abbey where Warwick the Kingmaker was buried as well as her brother, Warwick, and other members of the family.

Reginald played his own part in the escalating drama. When he came back from Paris in 1530 the king offered him either the bishopric of Winchester or the archbishopric of York which had both fallen vacant on the death of Cardinal Wolsey. Henry had approached Reginald already for support in his efforts to secure the annulment of his marriage to Katherine. Reginald knew that it would be very difficult for him personally to defy the king and to remain loyal to Rome so he declined both appointments and left the country.

Anne Boleyn's own fall allowed Margaret to return briefly to court in 1536 but this triumph was short lived for not long afterwards, the king received a copy of Reginald's letter, *De Unitate Ecclesiastica* (In Defence of the Unity of the Church). A cardinal now, Reginald's treatise was an attack on the royal supremacy, *i.e.* the king's undisputed authority now over spiritual matters in this country as set out in a series of measures enacted by parliament between 1531 and 1536. The king was not amused. He instructed Margaret to send Reginald a letter of rebuke but the reprimand could have been couched in stronger terms, and when word reached the king that Geoffrey Pole had been in communication with Reginald, the whole family stood accused of treasonable activity. Geoffrey was arrested in August 1538. Under interrogation and fearful of torture, he reported conversations with his brother Montagu and with their cousin Henry, marquess of Exeter. Montagu reportedly told Geoffrey:

> *I like well the doing of my brother Cardinal Pole. I would we were both overseas with the Bishop of Liege* [Reginald] *for this world will one day come to stripes. A time will come; I fear we shall not tarry the time. If we tarry the time we shall do well enough. It must needs come to this pass one day, and I fear me we shall lack nothing so much as honest men…I had liever dwell in the west parts than at Warblington, for in the west parts the marquis of Exeter is strong…*

Montagu and Exeter were arrested on 4 November. Found guilty of 'treasonable conversations', they were executed on Tower Hill on 9 December. Geoffrey was tried and found guilty on 4 December. He was condemned to death but was reprieved and released early in 1539.

Local men examined about the activities of the residents of Warblington Castle included Henry Holland of Warblington, a ship's master who had already been convicted of piracy. He was examined on 3 November 1529 and proved to be a useful source of information, confirming that from Warblington Castle, Montagu and others had sent frequent messages to their friends on the continent, especially Reginald, Cardinal Pole, using as agents people such as himself.

Holland informed his questioners that he had actually transported the vicar of Warblington to France. He hired a

Langstone harbour in 1856. This watercolour gives a good idea of what the creeks and channels of Langstone and Chichester harbours must have looked like in the early sixteenth century. PMRS

French ship and embarked his passengers - the vicar, his manservant, their horses and baggage including a substantial sum of money – at Portsmouth. They landed at Le Havre and he accompanied them to Paris. He left them in the company of two English students in Paris. Asked what communication he had with his passengers, he reported

> *the vicar told him he was glad he was over sea, for if he had tarried in England he feared he should have been put to death, for he considered the ordinances of England were against God's law.*

He was paid forty shillings subsequently by Sir Geoffrey Pole to carry letters to the vicar in Paris 'which he did'

> *and brought others home from the said vicar to Sir William Paulet, then Comptroller, Dr Stuarde, Chancellor to the bishop of Winchester, and to Sir Geoffrey Pole, and a little writing to the vicar's brother-in-law, John Fowell of Warblington, to whom he delivered also all the other letters to be conveyed to those men they were sent to...*

Geoffrey also sent for him when he heard that he was transporting a load of wheat to Flanders and asked him 'to get a message to the cardinal'. He alleged that Geoffrey said

> *I pray you to commend me to my brother and show him I would I were with him, and will come to him if he will have me; for show him the world in England waxeth all crooked, God's law is turned upso-down, abbeys [sic] and churches overthrown, and he is taken for a traitor; and I think they will cast down parish churches and all at the last*

He was also to alert Reginald that there was a price on his head, and that agents had been dispatched to France 'to kill him with a hand-gun or otherwise as they should see best'. He tracked down the cardinal finally in an abbey near Cambrai, gave him the messages and alerted him to the death threats.

It was damning material. Margaret was arrested at Warblington and her interrogation began there a few days later on 12 November, led by William Fitzwilliam, earl of Southampton and Thomas Goodrich, bishop of Ely. She stood her ground and refused to be intimidated. Afterwards

Fitzwilliam paid grudging tribute to her strength of character in a letter to the king's minister, Thomas Cromwell. However hard they questioned her, they could get nothing from her. They had to conclude that her sons had not made her privy to their activities 'or else is she the most errant traytresse that ever lived'. To the Privy Council, they reported; 'we have dealid with such a one as men have not dealid with to fore us, Wee may call hyr rather a strong and constaunt man than a woman'.

Initially she was removed to Cowdray House at Midhurst, Fitzwilliam's home. While there she was attainted of treason by parliament in May 1539 with her grandson, Montagu's son, Henry Vaughan. They were accused of aiding and abetting her sons, Montagu and Reginald, and of having committed 'diverse and sundrie other detestable and abhomynable treasons'. The evidence was thin and Cromwell worked hard to push her attainder through the House of Lords.

Warblington Castle had been searched thoroughly at the time of Margaret's arrest but Cromwell claimed now, some six months later, that a new search had uncovered in one of her coffers a tabard or tunic of white silk, embroidered on the front with the arms of England – three lions – and a wreath of pansies and marigolds, and on the back, with the Five Wounds.

The Five Wounds were in fact one of the devices of the Plantagenet coat of arms but unfortunately they had been used on the banners of the 'pilgrims' - the men and women of Lincolnshire and the north – whose resistance to the campaign against the monasteries in 1536 was known as the Pilgrimage of Grace. Margaret's family were not involved in the uprising but some of Montagu's comments at the time were construed as support. Margaret was now implicated as well.

Cromwell also alleged that the tunic was evidence of Reginald's intention to marry the Princess Mary and restore England to papal authority. Cromwell probably manufactured the evidence, or put a sinister interpretation on a perfectly innocent piece of clothing which may have belonged, quite reasonably, to Margaret's father. The evidence was enough to convince their lordships however. Her attainder passed finally through parliament and Margaret was despatched promptly to the Tower.

She was there for almost two years. She was in her late sixties now and perhaps the king hoped that if nature was allowed to take its course, he might not have to issue an unpopular and possibly, for him, unpalatable order to execute her. She was comparatively comfortable in the Tower. The king paid her a not ungenerous allowance for food and drink, and she had a waiting woman to attend her. However she always posed a threat to the king as a possible focus for rebellion, as had so many of her family before her, and when rebellion broke out again in the north of England in 1541, led by Sir John Neville, motivated in part by detestation of the royal supremacy, and when word reached the king and his ministers that Reginald was planning to rescue his mother, Henry and his ministers decided she had to go.

She was led out to her execution early on the morning of 27 May 1541. The circumstances were horrific. The official executioner was in the north dealing with the rebel leaders. Margaret was literally hacked to death by 'a wretched and blundering youth' in what was described as 'the most pitiful manner'. Her body lies buried in front of the altar in the chapel of St Peter ad Vincula in the Tower. When Reginald heard the news of his mother's death, he rejoiced that he was now the son of a martyr. Margaret was beatified by Pope Leo XIII in 1886 for her support for 'the truth of the orthodox faith'.

CHAPTER 3

Executed on the Quarterdeck
1757

The weather was miserable in Portsmouth on Monday morning 14 March 1757. The day did not begin too badly. The winds were moderate and it was hazy but in the latter part of the morning strong gales got up and, according to the log of HMS *Monarch*, there was rain. It was therefore with the utmost difficulty that the captains and officers of the men-of-war anchored at Spithead made their way in small boats across the open sea and into the harbour, in response to Admiralty orders that they attend on board *Monarch* by noon.

They were not alone on the water that morning. As well as the boats from the warships, the *Monarch* was surrounded by a mass of small craft seething with local people who were clearly there for some sort of sport or spectacle. They did not have long

Portsmouth in 1750. PMRS

to wait. While they would not have been able to see what was going on above their heads on board ship, they could not have failed to hear the volley of shots ring out at twelve noon when the Honourable John Byng, Admiral of the Blue, was shot dead by a marine firing squad, 'a martyr to political persecution', his family recorded bitterly on his tombstone in the parish church of Southill, Biggleswade, Bedfordshire.

They had every reason to feel bitter. John Byng is the only commander-in-chief in British history to have been executed by sentence of court-martial, and while some commanders have deserved to be court-martialled, Byng most certainly did not.

He was the fifth surviving son of the fifteen children of the naval hero, George Byng, first Viscount Torrington, and his wife Margaret Master, and was baptized on 29 October 1704. He went to sea under the tutelage of his uncle, Captain Streynsham, Master of the *Superb*, at the age of 14 in 1718, and took part in his father's great victory – the destruction of the Spanish fleet - off Cape Passaro that same year. He passed his lieutenant's examination in 1722 and by 1727 had been promoted to captain. His father was now First Lord of the Admiralty.

John Byng's progress thus far was enviable, and he might reasonably have expected in his declining years a similarly safe, comfortable, and profitable progress towards eventual retirement. He had a reputation for being proud and haughty but this may well have been the defence of a shy man – he never married - and he seems to have been something of a recluse although events would prove that his often stiff outward demeanour disguised a remarkable strength of character. He never had a wide circle of friends and when peace came in 1748 he returned to England, a vice-admiral now, and settled in his London house in Berkeley Street where he set about planning the construction of a country seat near Barnet in Hertfordshire. He had a companion now, a mistress called Mrs Hickson, about whom we know very little other than the fact that she was a poor widow, and below his rank socially, but, according to his family, he lived with her now discreetly and very happily. It was his great misfortune to be recalled to sea when hostilities loomed again in 1755.

He took command initially of the western squadron with orders to apprehend all French ships and their crews and send them to the nearest English port. The western squadron did its job well and was forced to return to land only by the most atrocious weather conditions in mid-November, which threatened to destroy its ships. Byng returned to London. Tragically Mrs Hickson died a few days after his return. Hopefully he received some consolation early the following year, when he was promoted to full admiral and charged to set sail from Spithead for the Mediterranean with orders to prevent the French from taking the island of Minorca.

It was a doomed expedition. He was sent far too late and with too few resources, and before he could get there, a strong French fleet arrived off Port Mahon and put ashore some fifteen thousand French troops who took the island with scarcely a shot fired in its defence. The vastly depleted British garrison, most of whose officers were in England on leave, retreated to Fort St Philip with the eighty-year-old acting governor, General Blakeney, and waited there for reinforcements.

In due course Byng did draw the French into a very gallantly fought action off Minorca which lasted over three hours. He succeeded in driving them off but his own ships received such a mauling that he was in no position to pursue or to put any men ashore to assist the beleaguered garrison. He believed that he had no alternative but to return to Gibraltar to put ashore his wounded and carry out repairs.

However, when he arrived finally in Gibraltar it was to learn there, on 3 July, that he and his second-in-command, Rear-Admiral West, were to be superseded by Vice-Admiral Sir Edward Hawke and Rear-Admiral Saunders. With Admiral West, he sailed for home only a few days later on 9 July on board the *Antelope*. They would be made scapegoats in due course, sacrificed, wrote a later commentator, 'to save the face of a government, and appease a populace stirred up to a high pitch of excitement by the lying propaganda organised by ministers of the crown'. It is an extraordinary statement and needs some explanation.

It is not a complicated story. Hostilities had been resumed in 1755 against the French and their allies, which included Spain and Austria, because of British fears of the growing influence of France in India and North America. There was also a very real fear at this time that the French might invade our shores.

British fears were exacerbated by the fact that during the preceding years of peace, very little money had been spent on defence. There was still a marked reluctance to spend money despite this new outbreak of hostilities and the Seven Years War, as it was called subsequently, saw limited resources spread very thinly over a wide field of military operations. In fact George II was so concerned for the safety of his own realm that he ordered the requisitioning of Hanoverian and Hessian troops to protect this country. The opposition and much of the country were outraged.

The threat of invasion was probably a bluff engineered by the French to keep British naval forces in home waters, and to distract attention from what was really going on in the Mediterranean in early 1756. There the French were assembling a strong fleet in their great base at Toulon but the king's ministers, led by the Duke of Newcastle, refused to recognise in these activities any threat to British interests on the nearby island of Minorca.

Minorca is the second largest of the Balearic group of islands midway between Marseilles and Algiers. It was valued particularly for its fine anchorage in the harbour at Port Mahon. It was captured from Spain in 1708 and within two years a useful naval base had been established there. Commanding the passage of naval and commercial shipping through the Mediterranean at this point, Minorca occupied a coveted and vital defensive position at the beginning of the Seven Years War. Newcastle and his fellow-ministers failed entirely to understand this and to take seriously the intelligence reports coming in from all directions alerting them to the threatened French invasion. Consequently they failed as well to take any steps to remedy the years of neglect of the island's defences and the weakness of the garrison.

They did not set out initially to destroy Byng but when the disastrous consequences of their own complacency and parsimony became clear they sought frantically to extricate themselves from the mire and to distribute blame for what happened elsewhere. It was unfortunate for all parties but particularly for Byng that the news of the loss of Minorca coincided with two serious defeats in North America. The government was roundly criticised on all sides for this string of disasters – by the opposition and by the City of London, which was concerned now for the safety of the country's trade routes, and needed to be placated as it supplied funds to prosecute the war. Equally vociferous were the general public who were outraged by these affronts to national pride. There was also an outraged monarch. The government needed to do something dramatic to placate these different critics.

Newcastle and his colleagues determined therefore to make an example of Byng and thus save their own skins. If truth had to be sacrificed along the way then that was the price they were prepared to pay. The government's propaganda machine swung into action with devastating effect. The initial account of the sea battle off Minorca to reach London had been a copy obtained by British intelligence sources of the highly-coloured account of what took place, written by the French commander-in-chief, the Marquis de la Gallissonniere. Far from recording that they had been forced to flee, he claimed that it was the British who had been obliged to retreat. On the strength of this missive – *the enemy's word* – the government ordered Byng's recall. When Byng's own report arrived, a good two weeks later and in advance of his return, the government sat on it for ten days before publishing a highly-edited version which omitted any words or passages which reflected flatteringly on Byng's own performance in the battle, and they let it be known that when he landed at Portsmouth he would be arrested, tried by court-martial and probably condemned to death.

The government also recruited the skills of the leading pamphleteers of the day to vilify Byng's reputation and thus distract public opinion from themselves. They were singularly successful. Byng's effigy was burnt in extraordinary public displays of hatred in many towns and villages.

The *Antelope* dropped anchor at Spithead on 26 July. Byng was put under close arrest immediately and, from that moment, treated like a felon. Whether it was planned deliberately or not, and if it was deliberate it was a particularly malicious piece of government engineering, the order for his arrest was brought to Byng by two members of his own family, his brother, Colonel Edward Byng, and Admiral Osborne, his brother-in-law. Edward was so upset by the whole business – his brother's arrest and the hatred and contempt of the Portsmouth mob – that he collapsed and died shortly afterwards while still on board the *Antelope*.

Byng was transferred shortly after his arrival from the *Antelope* to the *Royal Anne*, also lying in Portsmouth Harbour, and after being held there a week, he was taken to Greenwich by road with a strong escort of troops to protect him from any possible lynching parties, and of course to ensure that the government was not deprived of its scapegoat. He would be detained at Greenwich Hospital until his court-martial.

There indignity upon indignity was heaped upon his hapless head by the vindictive governor of the hospital. On his first night he was confined in a bare room with no furniture at all and was obliged to make what bed he could of his portmanteau and its contents. In due course his windows were secured by iron bars, and the chimney was blocked up to ensure that he did not try this unorthodox means of escape. Sentries were also posted outside his room day and night.

When he had asked with what he had been charged, he was told that *he did not do his utmost* either during the engagement or to relieve the garrison in Fort St Philip afterwards, and acted contrary to and in breach of his instructions. The charge was framed under the twelfth article of war which stated that

> *Every person in the fleet who through cowardice, negligence or disaffection, shall in time of action withdraw or keep back, or not come into the fight or engagement, or shall not do his utmost to take or destroy every ship, which it shall be his duty to engage, and to assist and relieve all and every of His Majesty's ships or those of his allies which it shall be his duty to assist and relieve; every such person so offending and being convicted thereof by the sentence of a court martial shall suffer death.*

Sitting isolated in his solitary room in Greenwich Hospital – some pieces of furniture were supplied in due course – Byng must have been utterly devastated. He believed unhesitatingly that he had a clear conscience, had done his duty and had used his utmost endeavours, in trying circumstances and with some success. This was his reward. There were many people who were uneasy about his plight, and his treatment. They included many of his fellow officers in the Mediterranean as well as both Fox and Pitt, but both these men, who might have done something to save Byng's life, were more concerned about the effect their support for him might have on their own future career prospects given the strength of public opinion.

One right-thinking fearless person who did come to Byng's support was Dr Samuel Johnson, who wrote several pamphlets countering successfully the scurrilous concoctions of the government's propagandists. He actually published the passages omitted so disgracefully from Byng's own account of the battle of Minorca and sought angrily to expose the machinations of Newcastle's ministry, but he was exceptional. As for the king, if he had any qualms, these were soon overcome as he assimilated the mood of the country and the placards on the streets addressed to the government with the warning 'Hang Byng, or mind your king.'

What the government and its propagandists had unleashed

on the streets like an evil genie was mob law. The mob had forced Newcastle and his fellow ministers to find a scapegoat to save their own skins in the first place and, out of the bottle now, the mob's clamour condemned Byng to his disgraceful death, and ensured that no one was brave enough to intervene to prevent this unfolding tragedy and travesty of justice.

Byng was brought back to Portsmouth for the court martial in a coach drawn by six horses flanked by fifty cavalry. He arrived in the town on 23 December. At every stage of the journey along the Portsmouth road the coach was set upon by crowds whipped up successfully by the excesses of the government's pamphleteers and prepared, given the opportunity, to drag him from the vehicle and lynch him then and there.

Once in Portsmouth he was provided with quarters in the dockyard in the house of Edward Hutchins, the Boatswain of the Dockyard. It was not a particularly pleasant billet. When the wind was in the north or north-west the house reeked of pitch from the great vats on Pitch House Jetty. The court martial began at nine o'clock on the morning of 28 December with the firing of a gun on board the *St George,* which had been prepared specially for the trial. Byng conducted his own defence calmly and efficiently, despite the hostility of the court and the disregard shown by the prosecution for the rules of evidence, as leading questions were put and hearsay evidence allowed. He cross-examined witnesses skilfully and with considerable effect. The weight of evidence was in his favour.

It fell essentially into three parts. Firstly, whether there had been any undue delay either before or after he got to Gibraltar, secondly how he had handled the fleet at Minorca and finally, whether it would have been possible either before or after the battle to land reinforcements or otherwise assist the beleaguered garrison.

His witnesses – those he was allowed to call for the government had limited the numbers – pointed out that he got his ships to sea in two weeks and to Minorca by 19 May which was an extraordinary feat given the lack of support he received in Portsmouth prior to his departure and the problems in the dockyard at Gibraltar where he had hoped to make good many of the deficiencies in his fleet. He also demonstrated successfully that while a number of sea-worthy and properly-manned ships had been retained at Portsmouth to counter the possible invasion, the ships allotted to him were the sweepings of the dockyard, less sea-worthy, inappropriately armed, under-manned, and without the contingent of marines which he might reasonably have expected to take on board before setting out for this particular theatre of war. They had to make way for the returning members of the garrison. Further, he had no hospital ship and no store ship.

His passage to Gibraltar was also held up by gales and then a calm, and when he reached Gibraltar finally the news that the French had landed troops on Minorca meant that he was delayed again, taking on board the supplies which would be unobtainable now on Minorca itself.

His efforts to get adequate supplies here were seriously frustrated and he sent a strongly-worded report on the inade-quacies of the Gibraltar dockyard back to England, which must have been unwelcome reading for the ministry on top of the news of the French landings, and may well have fuelled for the first time government antagonism towards him. However, the prosecution lawyers in the specially convened court on board the *St George* could elicit no support from witnesses for their contention that Byng had delayed unnecessarily on his way south. In fact, the evidence pointed to the contrary.

As for the contention that he had mishandled the disposition of the fleet during the battle, witnesses said that he got to close quarters quickly, and that the British attack was being pressed vigorously when the *Intrepid* was unluckily damaged aloft so badly that she was no longer manageable. Drifting, she endangered neighbouring ships astern which had to back their sails to avoid a collision. This endangered the flagship, *Ramillies*, which had to back as well. Only fifteen minutes of the battle was lost but in that time a large gap opened up between the van and the rear of the British fleet and Galissonniere tried to exploit this gap by cutting through the British line, but Byng managed to bring up the rear and frustrated the French, driving them back. Eventually, they pulled away and with cleaner, better-equipped ships, they outsailed the British and disappeared into the gathering dusk.

Despite the efforts of the prosecution, the witnesses called were in complete agreement that Byng did all that he could have done in a very critical situation. He drove off a far superior force and would have been justified in describing what took place as a British victory, and as for whether he could have landed reinforcements on Minorca, his own officers agreed that it would not have been possible and under cross-examination, General Blakeney himself agreed that even if the hoped-for detachment of troops had landed, he could not have saved the island.

An impartial set of judges would have been persuaded by the evidence thus far heard and would have dismissed the case but this court was not impartial, and was all too aware that their own futures depended on returning the verdict the government sought. They agreed that he was not responsible for the delays nor was he a coward but they found him guilty on the two counts of not doing his utmost either during the engagement or afterwards to assist the garrison, and he was sentenced to death, that being the consequence of a conviction under the twelfth article of war. However the court was extremely uneasy about this mandatory sentence and sent a unanimous plea for mercy to the Admiralty but to no avail. Despite the valiant efforts of his own family, led by his young nephew Lord Torrington and his sister, Sarah Osborne, who engaged in a furious correspondence with the Admiralty, as well as the support of such people as Horace Walpole and the French satirist, Voltaire, and even the French commander Gallissonniere, the sentence was upheld. On 14 March 1757 Admiral Byng was executed.

W G Gates quoted an anonymous account of what happened in his topographical notes in *Records of the Corporation 1928-1930*. Apparently, Byng had spent most of the time between eleven and twelve o'clock standing in the stern-walk of the *Monarch*, watching the crowds below with a telescope. He had actually said to one of his friends, 'I fear many of them will be disappointed – they may hear where they are, but they can't all see!' At noon he was told that all was ready:

> *To that he only replied by saying that he was glad that the tide would serve for his body to be taken ashore in the afternoon; adding that he was also glad to understand that there was apparently no disposition on the part of the Portsmouth people to insult it. The Admiral continued on his knees for rather more than a minute, amid an awful silence all round. He was quite composed, and kept his head bent, apparently in earnest prayer. Then he gave the signal to 'fire', by dropping a second handkerchief which he had held in his hand. The fatal volley went off on the instant. Five bullets struck Byng. The sixth passed over his head. He fell forward stone-dead.*

Byng's Execution. From Gates

Shortly afterwards Voltaire published his satirical novel, *Candide*. Landing at Portsmouth, Candide saw a stout gentleman on board a ship shot dead by a firing squad. He asked who this person might be and was told that it was an admiral. Candide was very curious and on inquiring further about this extraordinary incident was advised that in this country we kill the odd admiral occasionally 'to encourage the others'.

Byng's corpse was sent ashore the morning following his execution 'with all his Bagage [sic]', according to the log of HMS *Monarch*. Lake Allen, an early nineteenth century historian of Portsmouth considered, in his *History of Portsmouth* published in 1817, that Byng 'in his last moments conducted himself with a dignity and fortitude, that never inspired a breast infected with cowardice, or conscious of guilt.'

CHAPTER 4

Buster Crabb Disappears
1956

The disappearance of naval frogman Commander Lionel 'Buster' Crabb in Portsmouth Dockyard on 19 April 1956 at the age of forty-six remains one of the greatest Cold War mysteries and has produced more column inches of speculation than any other similar Cold War adventure. Few people are aware though, even locally, that he was buried or, to be strictly accurate, that the body that was identified by the Chichester coroner as that of Commander Crabb, was buried in Milton Cemetery in July 1957 after a requiem mass celebrated at St John's Roman Catholic Cathedral. 'At rest at last' reads the legend on the stone, placed on his grave by his mother.

Crabb's life and death are the stuff of screenplays. Even if he had not met an untimely end – as he seems to have done – in the cold waters of Portsmouth harbour in a maelstrom of unsought publicity, his wartime experiences alone deserve

St John's Roman Catholic Cathedral. From Gates

wider publicity, particularly as they also partially explain why he was in Portsmouth harbour that ill-fated morning.

He built up a formidable reputation as a diver in the Mediterranean between 1942 and the end of the Second World War. Marshall Pugh, who was working with him on a book about his wartime experiences when he died, wrote:

> *In November 1942 when Lionel Philip Kenneth Crabb was drawn into the battle against Italian frogmen, he was thirty-two years old, opposed to any form of exercise and capable of swimming only three lengths of a swimming-pool. He was to emerge from the struggle under water as a famous frogman and a minor legend of the Mediterranean war. He was to emerge still unable to swim more than one hundred yards without swimfins, with his deep dislike of exercise unimpaired.*

He had lived a restless peripatetic existence until the outbreak of war, never staying long in any job. A spell as an apprentice in the Merchant Navy had been followed by a brief period with Shell Eastern Petroleum in New York, and then a job with a cousin in an advertising syndicate back in London. He sold out his share though as soon as the business began to take off and set off round the world as a companion to his wealthy flat-mate whose addiction to alcohol had prompted his parents to send him on a cruise to the Far East. Crabb's instructions were to keep him from strong drink on the journey, and to lock him in his cabin when the ship went into port. However his companion had improved so much by the time they were due to return home that Crabb decided to abandon him and try his luck at business in Singapore but that did not work out and he returned to London. Odd jobs followed, including a spell as an assistant in an art gallery where he developed a life-long enthusiasm for modern art, particularly the works of Picasso. War was clearly looming though and he approached the Royal Naval Reserve (RNR) but they considered him too old at twenty-eight for their immediate purposes so he continued in the art gallery while studying naval gunnery in his spare time.

When war broke out finally the RNR still considered him too old so he signed on at the beginning of September 1939 as a merchant seaman gunner on a tanker bound for Aruba, then a Dutch possession in the Lesser Antilles in the West Indies. Twelve months later he transferred to the Royal Naval Patrol Service. He was commissioned at the end of 1941 but the Navy then discovered that he had a weakness in his left eye and he was barred from further service at sea. The only way he saw of getting back to service was by joining Mine and Bomb Disposal. After initial training and some experience gained in Swansea, he was sent to Gibraltar in November 1942.

Allied convoys of sometimes up to sixty ships would assemble in the Gibraltar roads at any one time, spreading out of necessity towards the Spanish coast. Some were anchored barely four hundred yards from Spanish beaches. Security was a nightmare. The ships were in full view of the Italian and German consulates in the neighbouring ports, and hundreds of dockyard workers came over daily from La Linea in Spain to work on the Rock. Besides possible risks of land attacks by Spain on Gibraltar itself, and the threats to the ships from German U-boats, proximity to Spain meant that it was very easy for Italian frogmen to harry allied ships by placing explosive devices below their waterlines with delayed timing mechanisms, and escape before the ships blew up.

Crabb's role as a mine-disposal officer was to make the devices retrieved safe. Initially it seemed a somewhat hopeless task. There were only two divers in Gibraltar when he arrived. They were neither professional divers nor were they mine-disposal people. They had no proper diving gear and they were up against the considerable skills and resources of the Tenth Light Flotilla of the Italian Navy, which had two very well-trained groups: the swimming group with flexible rubber suits, breathing gear and swimfins, or flippers as we call them today, and another group which was trained to man piloted torpedoes. These torpedoes were fourteen feet long with detachable warheads holding three hundred kilogrammes of explosive. Usually launched from a submarine, the pilot sat astride his torpedo with a diver behind him. When they reached their targets, the divers disconnected the warheads and attached them beneath the waterline with the time-fuse set. They then made a quick getaway, swimming to the nearest coast to await collection. Thus equipped, they were able to penetrate conventionally well-defended British harbours in the Mediterranean such as Gibraltar and wreak havoc.

The Tenth Flotilla's capacity to devastate shipping in Gibraltar had increased significantly by the end of 1942 when Crabb arrived there to take up his new duties. Under the unsuspecting eyes of the British they had managed to turn an Italian tanker, the *Olterra,* abandoned at Algeciras, barely four miles from Gibraltar, into a depot ship for their torpedoes. The torpedoes and their crews left the depot ship out of sight of any observer through a four-foot door six feet below the waterline.

Crabb was in Gibraltar only a short time before he decided that he had to join the divers beneath the waves. They had no rubber suits, only naval overalls or their swimming trunks, and weighted gym shoes with ill-fitting goggles. He made his first dive in late November and discovered his first limpet mine early the following month. The pressure from the Tenth Flotilla did not let up throughout this time and it was clear now to the naval authorities that they would have to expand their tiny team of divers if they were to have any hope of defending allied shipping effectively.

The Underwater Working Party, as it was named, was established in the New Year, and recruits were sought by the diving officer, Lieutenant Bailey, and Crabb from ships and shore establishments in Gibraltar. Competition was keen and a number of skilled and doughty individuals were recruited, including several who subsequently made their homes in Portsmouth. They included Chief Petty Officer Thorpe who brought to the team his specific knowledge of escape apparatus, acquired training submariners. According to Marshall Pugh, once it was established, the Underwater Working Party

> had the usual high morale of a special show. The legend of how Bailey and Crabb had dealt with mines and enemy frogmen grew as the Party ratings went slumming among men of lesser outfits. The ratings smiled among themselves when outsiders asked them about 'Buster' Crabb. The rating divers had heard from the diving-launch crew about the first limpet-mine and, watching Crabb, they became convinced that he was incapable of fear.

When the team was fully trained they searched ships day and night, examining whole convoys, often in complete darkness. The Tenth Flotilla's capacity to inflict awful damage was still undiminished however and when in May 1943 they managed to destroy the United States Liberty ship, *Pat Harrison,* and two British ships, *Mahsud* and *Camerata,* Bailey and Crabb began to suspect that the *Olterra* might have something to do with the success of these raids and offered to do a little snooping round that ship. They were forbidden to do so however by the intelligence and security services and more terrible damage was inflicted on allied shipping, including the British steamer *Stanridge,* the Norwegian tanker *Thoshovdi* and the American Liberty Ship *Harrison Gray Otis* in August by three piloted torpedoes.

When the Polish military leader, General Sikorsky's plane, carrying him to England from the Middle East, crashed into the water just beyond the end of the Gibraltar runway Bailey and Crabb were sent into the water the following day to see if they could recover his papers in case they were washed ashore in Spain. They found the general's brief-case and broken bags of microfilm mail intended for home by soldiers in the Middle East. Every scrap of paper and film was retrieved from the wrecked plane.

Bailey and Crabb's personal war with the Italian Tenth Flotilla came to an end unexpectedly on 8 September 1943, when Italy asked for an armistice. The flotilla broke up. Some men joined and fought on land on the Republican side. Others made their way south to join the advancing allies. The abandoned *Olterra* was now towed into Gibraltar. As Crabb had suspected, evidence was discovered of the activities of the Tenth Flotilla. A piloted torpedo was found in the wreckage and, of course, the underwater dock.

For his work in Gibraltar Crabb was awarded the George Medal and promoted to Lieutenant-Commander. He was sent to Italy in mid-summer 1944 to join what Marshall Pugh described as a 'rugged outfit' known as the Joint Services Intelligence Collecting Unit, which was made up of Americans and British from all three fighting services. When the allies entered Florence the unit was instructed to seize important enemy weapons, equipment and documents, and individual officers were charged to search for information in their own particular fields of expertise. Crabb had been despatched from Leghorn to join the unit as an expert on the Italian Tenth Light Flotilla. Mines were also made in Florence and he would bring his own knowledge of this branch of warfare to the table.

In due course he would be placed in command of all anti-sabotage diving operations in northern Italy with overall command of bomb safety parties on both coasts so that he could co-ordinate activities. As ever there was a serious shortage of shallow-water divers but help came from an unexpected quarter as a number of former members of the Italian Tenth Flotilla, which had not been entirely broken up and dispersed after all, came over very amicably to the allied side and joined his clearance-diving team. They found themselves in the very curious situation of swimming round American ships in allied ports looking for mines placed by men of their old unit.

After a protracted spell in hospital with jaundice in early 1945, Crabb was sent to join the token naval force assembling at Ancona to enter Venice as bomb-safety officer, and in due course he did indeed lead the naval force into Venice on 29 April 1945 where they were billeted initially in the Danieli Hotel. Crabb had not wanted to be in Venice. He suspected that he was being rested and given lighter duties because of his recent illness but luck was on his side. From conversations with the Partisan liaison officer, and information obtained from certain prisoners held in the Naval Academy, he and his American counterpart, Lieutenant Tony Marsloe of the United States Navy, learnt that to the north-east of the Lido on the small island of Le Vignole was a Republican base for training German frogmen in piloted torpedoes.

The workshops and laboratories were intact and there was a terrific range of Tenth Flotilla equipment still in store, guarded jealously by two sergeants who had refused to retreat with the Germans because they did not want the equipment to fall into the hands of the Partisans. They professed to be quite happy to surrender to Anglo-American forces however. They knew of Crabb and shook him warmly by the hand when he arrived with Marsloe to investigate, for they were desperately anxious to retrieve their beloved torpedoes from the canals where the Germans had sunk them in the middle of the night just before they left. The sergeants had watched what was going on from cover and were quite convinced that the Germans planned to come back as a sabotage party and use the machines against allied shipping.

With official blessing Crabb and Marsloe took over Le Vignole. Their brief was to assess the value of the equipment there and the experiments which had been under way, and then use the place to carry out experiments of their own. They were ably assisted in this enterprise by the veteran First World War submariner, Commander Angelo Belloni, who was languishing in a local jail when they first arrived. Belloni had established the Tenth Light Flotilla, invented and supervised the manufacture of much of its equipment, and persuaded Mussolini of its possibilities. As Marshall Pugh puts it neatly:

> the swimmers of the Gamma Group had worn Belloni diving-suits and Belloni breathing-gear. Belloni was Crabb's most important enemy.

Crabb and Marsloe got the old man out of jail and installed him on Le Vignole, where he did indeed became Crabb's most important prisoner of the war. In the meantime his team of mainly Italian divers – the Royal Naval Clearance Diving Team, Venice - worked urgently to clear the adjacent sea and canals of Venice of mines. It was a difficult and dangerous enterprise which could be undertaken only by divers. Minesweepers making their way in from the sea dared not risk exploding mines close inshore for fear of damaging the city's historic fabric. For his services in opening up the port of Venice to shipping, Crabb was appointed Member of the Most Excellent Order of the British Empire (OBE).

At Christmas 1945 Crabb was flown down to Naples with his diving-gear to be briefed by the Commander – in – Chief Mediterranean, Sir John Cunningham, who asked him to fly to Haifa and form there an underwater working party similar to those he had set up in Gibraltar and Leghorn. Jewish underground organisations were determined to get rid of the British, and a number of large British police launches had been blown up by underwater mines. He established the diving team and trained a party on each naval ship to be able to examine the keel of their ship and take off a mine in an emergency. There was a lull now in underwater sabotage in Israel, and he was sent back to Italy charged to hand over Le Vignole to the Italian navy and to return to Haifa as soon as possible. He did not enjoy his time in Israel. It was 'tedious and dangerous, like unending flight in an unsafe aeroplane', according to Marshall Pugh. He learnt towards the end of his posting that he had been high on a terrorist assassination list. He returned to England and was demobbed finally in Portsmouth in Spring 1948.

It is difficult to be sure exactly what Crabb did next. If he did transfer to underwater espionage he would not have advertised the fact and it would have suited his purposes well, and those of military intelligence, if he was able to convince close friends and former colleagues that, like many men with similar backgrounds, he found it difficult to settle down in drab post-war Britain. According to Marshall Pugh, he desperately wanted a career as a civilian shallow water diver but no opportunities came his way and he made ends meet with an assortment of jobs, mainly in the printing and publishing business, but these activities were hampered by the acute paper shortage. He began developing an interest however in the possibilities of underwater photography. It was good cover if he was indeed a new intelligence recruit.

He told Pugh when they were working on his biography that he paid a visit to the Admiralty Research Laboratory at Teddington, where he saw lengths of film taken by James Hodges who had served in midget submarines on D Day and who, as a civilian, was experimenting with underwater cameras. He, Crabb, suggested the films should be edited and worked up into one film. It was agreed. He wrote a script for the film and it went out to the public as *Wonders of the Deep*. On the strength of this success he was apparently offered a job in underwater photography at Teddington early in 1949 to experiment with underwater photography and lighting. He began diving with Hodges to photograph wrecks in harbours, and to help salvage divers before they began work; to film the behaviour of underwater weapons and equipment, and to experiment with new cameras and lights, and new breathing equipment and diving-suits. It was apparently secret and important work and again, splendid cover for espionage.

He and Hodges played a key role in attempts to rescue the men of H M Submarine *Truculent*, which went down in the Thames estuary on 12 January 1950, sunk in an accident by the Swedish ship *Divina*. Later in the same year he took part in a Royal Navy clearance-diving team training exercise to search for a sixteenth century Spanish galleon, sunk in Tobermory bay off the Isle of Mull in the storms which beset Philip of Spain's Armada fleet in 1588. In due course he was recalled officially to the Navy. He appears in the Navy Lists of 1955 and 1956 as Commander (Special Branch) L K P Crabb RNVR GM OBE HMS *Vernon*. HMS *Vernon* was the Underwater Countermeasures and Weapons Establishment at Portsmouth.

But throughout this period Crabb seems to have convinced many of his friends and former colleagues that he was no different from them and, like them, facing up to the harsh reality of having to find a job and make a living shortly in 'civvie' street. A few were aware though that all might not have been what it seemed. Pugh's book was published after Crabb's disappearance, later in 1956, and he was clearly one of those who was aware then that Crabb was engaged in clandestine activities during these years. He wrote that occasionally

Crabb would set off on an outing for Portsmouth and be unusually vague about his intentions. For his Portsmouth trips he had an almost ceremonial rig: fawn tweed suit, pork-pie hat, and...sword-stick. In Portsmouth there was also an

almost ceremonial joke. Naval diving friends who suspected that he had arrived on mysterious business would say, 'Hullo, Crabbie. Something on?'

And he would reply, 'Just dropped down for a haircut and shave'.

Once one of his old colleagues suggested that I should help to persuade him to 'stop this underwater business. He's done enough in his time'. I did not know what the 'underwater business' was, and, by his gentle evasions, Crabb made it clear that it was no business of mine. The thought of Military Intelligence work did not occur to me, and I attached no particular significance to the fact in Coronation Year, Crabb had done some unusual underwater job in the Canal Zone and, on return to England, had reported immediately to the C.-in-C. Mediterranean, who was, of course, at that time in England.

Despite Navy List evidence to the contrary, Pugh maintains that by the end of 1955 Crabb was working for an old acquaintance as office manager of an organisation which supplied furnishings for espresso coffee bars. One night he said that he might want to borrow Pugh's car for 'a little job down in Portsmouth about the middle of April'. He was particularly brisk and cheerful that night, Pugh wrote. He never saw him again.

Crabb disappeared, diving, on 18-19 April 1956. The Admiralty issued a statement on 29 April saying that Commander Crabb was

missing, presumed dead after failing to return from an underwater trial. He did not return from a test dive which took place in connection with trials of certain under-water apparatus in Stokes bay, in the Portsmouth area, about a week ago.

At the time of his disappearance, three Russian warships were alongside the South Railway Jetty in Portsmouth dockyard. They had brought Soviet leaders Nikita Kruschev and Marshal Nikolai Bulganin to this country for very high level talks. Two days after their departure, the Admiralty issued its statement. On 4 May a Russian Assistant Naval Attaché in London said that a frogman had been seen near one of the ships, the *Ordzhonikidze,* in the harbour. A protest note was delivered to

Miscellaneous cuttings from The News, Portsmouth relating
to Commander Crabb.

the British Ambassador in Moscow. The Prime Minister, Sir
Anthony Eden, expressed regret about the incident in a return
note to the Soviet Government. On 9 May in the House of
Commons he said in a statement:

> It would not be in the public interest to disclose the circum-
> stances in which Commander Crabb is presumed to have met
> his death. While it is the practise for Ministers to accept
> responsibility, I think it necessary in the special circumstances
> of this case, to make it clear that what was done was done
> without the authority or the knowledge of her Majesty's

Ministers. Appropriate disciplinary steps are being taken.

The Opposition asked for an adjournment of the House to debate the matter but the Speaker ruled that it was 'on the grounds of public interest' that the Prime Minister could not add to his statement. The local and national press were in agreement that the Prime Minister's statement was very odd indeed. Brushing aside the references to Stokes Bay in the Admiralty's original statement for the smokescreen they clearly were, they asked why, if Crabb had dived near the *Ordzhonikidze* as a civilian, it was the Admiralty which announced his presumed death? Further, they pointed out, the Prime Minister said that it was against the public interest to reveal what was going on yet, what was done was done without authority or knowledge of either him or his fellow ministers *and disciplinary action would be taken.*

The Daily Herald warmed to this theme on 10 May. The Prime Minister, it said, won't say who is being disciplined or how or why. Is it for ordering Crabb to dive, for not telling the Prime Minister, or whether someone at the Admiralty is in hot water for making a blundering announcement of Crabb's death? The public can only draw its own conclusions, it opined. Further, it continued, the Prime Minister's lips are sealed at a time when we, the public, can only conclude that our security services were spying on his Russian guests without his knowledge. This will hardly improve our relations with the Russians, the paper suggested, or impress the Americans. It also suggested that such statements did not scotch rumours. Rather, they lead to more! By such 'hush-hush' tactics, it continued, the Prime Minister was getting into another Burgess and Maclean scandal, in which the truth will have to come out eventually, however shocking it is. It would be far better, the paper said, to speak out frankly now and end all the mystery. 'Secrecy is futile, and it is the way to make suspicions grow'.

And grow they did as all inquiries about Crabb's disappearance came up against a wall of official secrecy. The one real fact was that nobody wanted to talk about it. Suspicions were further fuelled when it emerged that a Portsmouth police officer took away several pages of the register of the *Sallyport* Hotel where Crabb had stayed the night before his last dive. It was known that Crabb went to Portsmouth with another man, called Smith, and that they both signed in at the *Sallyport*. The evidence had now been removed.

Amongst the initial theories put forward to account for Crabb's disappearance was the simple suggestion that he had trouble with his equipment after diving near the Russian ships and was asphyxiated. Others suggested that he was seen by the Russians – they had, after all, reported that they saw a diver – and that he was taken on board one of their ships before he died. His body was then replaced in the water. The most likely theory advanced was that after being seen by the Russians in the water he met with some mishap, and was trapped either deliberately or accidentally by an underwater object. As for why he was diving, it was suggested plausibly that he was working privately for an intelligence organisation either of this country or another NATO member or, that he was experimenting on behalf of a company interested commercially in underwater operations.

Meanwhile many of his former colleagues now living in the Portsmouth area were testifying movingly to journalists about the man they described as 'completely fearless' who 'devoted his life to diving' and would never ask a man to do what he was not prepared to do himself. A sailor who had worked with him at the San Andrea torpedo base in Venice spoke admiringly of the personality who was able to persuade captured Italians to work for the British in clearing harbours:

> How he managed it I just don't know. He got them rations, and even cigarettes 'on the quiet' and in the end they almost worshipped him. They accomplished near impossibilities in clearing the harbour.

Another spoke about Crabb's 'belligerent' appreciation of Picasso and his works, and how he loved fast driving.

Stories proliferated from the beginning, usually originating in the foreign press, that Crabb was alive and well, or certainly alive, usually in the Eastern bloc. Typical was the report in the West German newspaper *Bild Zeitung*, which said that Crabb was a prisoner in Moscow's Lefortowo prison awaiting trial for espionage. It quoted a French left-wing politician who had returned recently from the Soviet Union as saying that Crabb was taken to Moscow after being arrested by Soviet frogmen in Portsmouth harbour on 19 April. The French Socialist party and the head of its recent delegation to Moscow subsequently denied that any of their delegation had been so informed!

And for lack of any further copy or leads, the story of Commander Crabb's disappearance faded from the headlines until, in early February 1957, a local man, Harry Cole, of Emsworth, reported that in July the previous year, fishing late at night in Chichester Harbour, he had felt a terrific weight on his trawl. He stopped and pulled it in, thinking that he had caught a giant skate on the front of the trawl. As he grabbed the 'thing' he realized suddenly that he had a head in his hands:

> *I dropped it, but kept hold of a mouthpiece, tube, a piece of metal, and a belt which goes around a man's chest.*

> *The head and the body dropped away straight down to the seabed. I dropped the trawl again to hold the boat's position and took a two-point compass bearing from the Nab Tower and the light on Hayling Island Yacht Club.*

Astonishingly, he did not report his discovery for well over six months, by which time it was too late for the police to organise a search. However, a few months later, in June, a body reappeared, headless and in a frogman's rubber suit, floating 250 yards offshore in Prinsted Channel. It was discovered by three men fishing. 'We first saw the body floating a few inches below the water', they reported, 'a long, thin body in a close-fitting grey-black rubber suit with flippers'. Formal identification of the body was extremely difficult. The head was missing. So too were the hands and it had been in the water so many months that it was practically destroyed from the waist up. The Chichester coroner, Mr GF Bridgeman, concluded that the body was Commander Crabb's:

> *They had been told by witnesses that Commander Crabb was a small man, that he had a deformity of the toes, a scar on the left knee and that he wore a special type of underwater equipment, and Mrs Crabb had said that the hairs on his body were ginger.*

> *All this evidence pointed to the fact that this was Commander Crabb's body, and in support was the evidence of Superintendent Alan Hoare that no other frogman was missing in South Coast waters*

He recorded an open verdict. Curiously, no evidence was given at the inquest about the last two days of Crabb's life. The man who signed the register at the *Sallyport* as a Mr Smith, who was said to be with Crabb, and paid the bill after Crabb vanished, was not called to give any evidence. The coroner did not pursue Portsmouth's Chief Constable, Mr Arthur West, either, and ask why a Portsmouth policeman was sent to the hotel to remove the pages of the register which contained the signatures of both Crabb and his companion. He did not do so because it is clear from papers released almost forty years later by the Public Record Office that he had been asked not to. In short he had been briefed either by those organisations that had been responsible for putting Crabb into the water early on the morning of 19 April 1956, when the Russian ships were alongside the South Railway Jetty in Portsmouth harbour or by those charged to organise the cover-up.

As the years passed some additional information was divulged by individuals who had been involved in events at the time but much reporting was still highly speculative. Typical was a series of articles which appeared in *The News* in 1974. The author of the articles, John Stretton, suggests that there was genuine fear in the 1950s of the threat to Western navies of nuclear mines. Could cruisers such as the *Ordzhonikidze* have hatches in their hulls through which these mines could be dropped? He goes on to say with some certainty that the intelligence services decided to have a look at her hull while *Ordzhonikidze* was in Portsmouth, and while Stretton does not discuss Crabb's wartime experiences in Gibraltar of the hatch on the *Olterra,* this must have been a factor in Crabb being asked to undertake this particular diving mission.

Stretton did interview Arthur West though. He was living in retirement by then in Ramsgate in Kent. The Chief Constable had been involved originally in making security arrangements for the Russian visitors with Russian Security, the MVD, known later as the KGB. The parties had met in his offices at Byculla House in Queen's Crescent, Southsea, then Portsmouth City Police's headquarters building. Known today by its original name of 'Brankesmere', it is now a local architect's practice and private homes.

On the day before the Russian ships berthed, Crabb and another man, Mr Bernard Smith, according to West, whom Stretton describes as 'the young agent assigned to the case', then aged 31 and an Oxford graduate fluent in Russian and German, turned up at Byculla. West told Stretton:

> *They told me they were working for the Secret Service and that their mission was to examine the bottom of the Ordzhonikidze.*

*Smith said it was thought the hull was sheathed in stainless
steel and was thus resistant to marine life and mines.
At that time it was a plausible story. I later learned that the
ship had been examined once before, already, in the Baltic.*

West also believed that a new diving suit was being tested which
had pockets for weights across the shoulders and he told
Stretton that

*Smith told me when he returned from the mission that when
Crabb came back to Kings Stairs it was to adjust the weights.
He told Smith he was too light and wanted further weights put
in the suit. I imagine that the additional weights made the suit
too heavy and Crabb drowned.*

Before he agreed to help the two strangers West said that he
checked their credentials with MI 5, who confirmed that they were
who they said they were, and that their mission was as they had
outlined. The Chief Constable gave them an office in Central
Police Station with a scrambler telephone and assigned a local
policeman, Superintendent Lamport, to look after them. It was
Lamport who removed the pages from the register at the *Sallyport*
hotel. Stretton accepts West's theory that Crabb drowned, and in
an article published two years later in 1976, when another Russian
ship was visiting Portsmouth, he repeats this assertion in a lively
account of events on the morning Crabb disappeared:

*Smith and Crabb walked to the Dockyard on the fateful day
of April 19. They showed passes at the main gate and went
quickly to Kings Stairs.*

*Crabb slipped off outer clothing. To the frogman's suit he was
wearing underneath he added flippers and a special breathing
set that would leave no tell-tale bubbles.*

*Within a few minutes of entering the murky water, he was
back. The sky was lightening as he told Smith he had been
under the Russian ships…but hadn't completed the inspection
because he was having trouble with his equipment.*

*Smith helped him adjust the weights in the pockets of the
wetsuit and the oxygen re-breathing gear, and then Crabb was
gone.*

The minutes passed. But there was no sign of the ageing diver. Smith waited nearly an hour in an agony of suspense and worry. Then he gathered up Crabb's clothes and got out of the Dockyard.

At 9 am he burst into Chief Constable West's office and gasped: 'We've lost Crabb'. Mr West was decisive. He ordered Supt. Lamport to contact MI 5 for instructions. Lamport's orders were explicit...

He went to the Sallyport Hotel and removed the evidence of Smith and Crabb's short occupation, by tearing four pages from the hotel register. Within a few hours Smith was reporting, shamefacedly, to his SIS superiors.

There was little to add to the story until, in 1999, documents released by the Public Record Office, now The National Archives, under the thirty year rule, indicate that, as many had suspected, Crabb was engaged in an official covert mission. Government ministers may not have been aware of what was going on but the intelligence services most certainly were. They had commissioned him. The speculation in the newspapers at the time was right. Crabb was there to spy on the Soviet warships. A full investigation into what happened did take place and there was a thorough review of the military's espionage methods. Before Crabb's disappearance the military had a free hand to spy on Russian naval forces whenever they wished without securing government approval first. Henceforward ministers had to be briefed on any proposed spying missions.

It is also clear that the Prime Minister was seriously embarrassed by the incident, all the more so as the naval authorities in Portsmouth had assured the Russians when the diver was first seen swimming between their ships that no diving operations were being carried out in the area. Crabb's intelligence service handlers were also severely criticised in a report obtained by BBC Radio Solent with a Freedom of Information application early in 2006. The report showed that they did not take proper precautions to protect either him or the secrecy of the mission. A further tranche of material was released by the National Archives later in 2006. These papers make clear that it was certainly not the Royal Navy which sent Crabb on his last mission. The Navy was in fact shocked and embarrassed by what had happened not least because these documents show that one of their own officers had been caught up in the incident.

The unidentified officer took Crabb out in a small boat and stayed onboard while he dived. The officer said in his secret account of events that he had been asked to assist Crabb 'entirely unofficially and in a strictly private capacity'. He said that Crabb was carrying sufficient oxygen for an absence of a maximum of two hours submerged and that his actions until his disappearance under the surface were entirely normal. The conditions for diving were good.

The Navy was very keen that this man should not appear at the inquest in Chichester as his story would not have been consistent with the impression they were being obliged to convey that this had been a naval operation. If it had been a genuine naval operation there would have been 'immediate and extensive rescue operations'. The anonymous diver would also have taken action. In the circumstances – alongside the Russian ships – this was not possible. He was ordered to return to his ship and take no further part in the incident. The Navy was more than aware that this laid them open, singly and severally, to charges of 'negligence, lack of humanity and error of judgement'.

A temporary clerical officer was sent to Chichester to represent the Admiralty at the inquest. As one of the documents explains, he 'knows nothing of the background to the story and will not be able to answer any embarrassing questions even if they are asked'. The same document also reveals that the coroner had been made aware of the background of the case 'and is not asking for the appearance of any embarrassing naval witnesses'.

Further classified documents released at the end of 2007 reveal that ministers actually ordered Admiralty staff to lie about what happened. It is here, in hitherto secret documents, that government spokesmen and their press officers were instructed to say that Crabb had been killed while working on an experimental mine in Stokes Bay and, if pressed, that this incident had nothing whatsoever to do with the visit of the Russian ships. They were advised to avoid getting involved in any further detailed discussions on the subject 'because we can think of no answer which would not involve telling lies which might be exposed... .'

When journalists discovered that pages from the *Sallyport*

Hotel register had been torn from the book the Admiralty press team was advised to blame local police who had acted on their own initiative. This whole line of argument had of course to be changed a few days later when the Russians announced that one of their seamen saw a frogman surface near to their ship. Press officers were told now to say that it was unlikely that this was Crabb and, if asked whether he might have been murdered, to answer: 'I cannot believe in these possibilities'.

What actually happened to Crabb has never emerged. The theories are legion ranging from the Chief Constable's conjecture that the additional weights on his diving suit prevented him getting back to the surface in time to the suggestions that he was either caught up on something beneath the surface or was apprehended in some other way beneath the hulls of the Russian ships. The rust marks found on the rubber diving suit of the body pulled from the water in Prinsted Channel might well indicate that its owner got caught up in a piece of long-abandoned equipment on the sea bed.

However, a former head of Soviet Naval Intelligence now living in Israel claims that Crabb was shot dead in Portsmouth harbour by a Russian marksman. A Russian television documentary claims that Crabb was captured and killed by Soviet divers when he was placing an explosive device on one of their ships.

Even if the Government does know what happened to Crabb, ministers decided some time ago that the incident is still politically sensitive. Cabinet papers will therefore remain sealed until 2057, either to spare future government embarrassment or to protect someone's reputation. Don Hale, in his book *The Last Dive*, published in 2007, suggests that Lord Mountbatten may have had a role in the drama. In the meantime, someone still tends Crabb's grave in Milton Cemetery.

NAVAL AND MILITARY

CHAPTER 5

Portsmouth Captured for Parliament

1642

Portsmouth City Council possesses one of the finest collections of civic plate in the country, ranking in importance behind only London and Norwich. The bulk of the collection was accumulated over a short one hundred year period between the late sixteenth and late seventeenth centuries when it was usual for new councillors and other prominent individuals newly-arrived in the town to present a piece of plate to the corporation.

The collection includes a number of remarkable pieces: the early sixteenth century silver-gilt Bodkin Cup and the fabulous Lee Cup which bears a London hallmark of 1590. Its companion piece, the Ducie Cup, is in the Hermitage Museum in St Petersburg. These pieces have survived for one reason only – the ignominious defeat early in the Civil War of Portsmouth's royalist garrison by Parliamentary forces, and the town's subsequent withdrawal from the conflict for the duration of the war. Other cities, such as nearby Chichester and, further afield, Oxford, who were engaged longer in the fighting, saw their civic silver seized and melted down for ready money.

The Earl of Clarendon in his *History of the Great Rebellion* described Portsmouth in 1642 as 'the strongest and best fortified town in the kingdom' and it was clear to both sides – the Royalists and Parliament - that it was an important prize as both a garrison and a royal dockyard. For the king in particular Portsmouth was important as

Colonel George Goring. From Gates

a military headquarters in the south, and as a possible gateway for men and supplies from his friends abroad.

The Governor of Portsmouth was Colonel George Goring. He was thirty-four years old and the son of Baron Goring who became Earl of Norwich in due course. He had gained some military experience in France and later, in the wars in the Low Countries where he had been wounded in the ankle and permanently lamed at the Siege of Breda in 1637. However this had not prevented him from serving in the two recent and somewhat inglorious campaigns against the Scots and he was now the man charged with deciding which side Portsmouth would support in the coming war.

He enjoyed a dubious reputation. He had dissipated his wife's not inconsiderable dowry in the early years of their marriage and accumulated formidable debts. Clarendon described him as 'devious, uncertain, and unprincipled', and a man who 'shed disgrace upon the nobleness of his name, and upon the honourable profession of soldier'. Further, he wrote:

> *on account of his private vices of drunkenness, cruelty, and rapacity, and of his political timidity and treachery, scarcely anyone was more unworthy to be trusted with any important matters for counsel or execution.*

Few more recent commentators have seen fit to disagree seriously with these sentiments and certainly his behaviour in Portsmouth as garrison commander in the year before the outbreak of hostilities showed him in a particularly poor light.

There was one story which involved their own governor, the Earl of Portland, and scandalised the people of Newport on the Isle of Wight. It is recounted by W H Long in his introduction to the Oglander Memoirs:

> *the sight of their worshipful governor with his boon companions Hicks, Nicholas Weston and the dissolute Colonel Goring, Governor of Portsmouth, marching in drunken revelry towards the town gallows. At each health they drank they tore each others' bands and raiment, till by the time they reached their destination their clothes and shirts were in tatters. Then Goring mounted the ladder, and, with tipsy gravity, delivered his last dying speech to the bystanders, advising them all to take warning by his unhappy end. It had been better for himself and his fame if his wretched buffoonery had been stern reality.*

He was in fact a favourite of Queen Henrietta Maria, and he reassured her during 1641 that in an emergency he would put Portsmouth at her disposal as a place of refuge, and with a group of discontented army officers, he plotted to give the king military support if his position weakened further. But when he learnt that there was no guarantee that he would be made Lieutenant-General, he revealed the details of the plot to leading figures in the House of Lords – while still maintaining contact with the dissident army officers.

Early in May the veteran politician John Pym, who had been informed of the plot, briefed his fellow-Parliamentarians, and the details of the conspiracy were made public. The poor queen however was quite unaware of Goring's treachery, and decided now to put herself under his protection. She was only dissuaded from doing so at the last minute when she was apprised finally of the brutal facts. Remarkably Goring survived the Commons inquiry into the affair and was confirmed in his governorship of Portsmouth.

There was no reason to believe now that the town was not firmly on Parliament's side which must have been a great relief to local merchants and all those who derived their income from supplying the fleet, which was controlled by Parliament. It would be rash in the extreme to fall out with this side. But during the last months of 1641 it seems that some anonymous letters were sent by individuals in the Portsmouth area to the Commons alleging that Goring was in secret contact again with the king's side. It was true. He assured the king of his continued loyalty despite appearances to the contrary and, astonishingly, he was believed! To money coming from Parliament to make good defects in the town's defences came money now from the Royalist side for military expenses. The queen herself sold plate and jewels in order to send him money herself.

Not surprisingly, Goring was summoned to London by Parliament to explain the anonymous letters himself. However, a bravura performance before his fellow MPs – he was the Member now for Portsmouth – convinced them that there was nothing amiss. His plans for the landward defences were roundly approved, and he was paid the arrears of costs due him. According to Clarendon, he was also given an undertaking 'that he should be Lieutenant-General of the horse in their new army when it should be formed'.

Throughout the Spring and early Summer of 1642 Parliament had no further reason to doubt his loyalty, nor did the king for Goring received orders from Charles in York in mid-June commanding him to safeguard the town of Portsmouth and its magazine. He was charged to seize the pinnace, the *Henrietta Maria,* and use the ship and its guns as he saw fit to stave off attack, and to build fortifications wherever he saw fit on Portsea Island. He was also advised to raise officers and men as necessary to deal with any dangers.

Clearly the king was aware that the people of Portsmouth themselves favoured the parliamentary cause for he warned Goring to be careful 'for preventing of mutiny within the said town' by ensuring that he let no disaffected persons either reside in the town or be employed in the garrison. Later dispatches repeated these instructions. Finally, in mid-July, Goring threw over Parliament and made public his undivided allegiance to the Crown.

The Earl of Clarendon maintained that Goring's declaration precipitated the country into full-scale war. It certainly outraged his erstwhile parliamentary colleagues, despite the fact that rumours had been rife in the days preceding his announcement that he was in touch with the king's men. They were particularly annoyed that they had only recently issued warrants for the payment of £5,000 for garrison purposes.

According to a contemporary pamphleteer, on 2 August Goring first summoned the garrison to assemble, probably on the parade ground. Mindful of the advice he had received from the king on preventing mutiny, he promised to make good all arrears of pay if the men would swear an oath of loyalty to the Crown. If they were not prepared to do so they were at liberty to go. Some were delighted to subscribe to the oath but there were a substantial number who were not prepared to do so. The mayor and his fellow townsmen were summoned next and exhorted to make a similar declaration of loyalty. Information is limited on how many were prepared to swear such an oath. A newsletter published a few days later by Parliament stated that the town proposed to stand firm in its obedience to that body and to oppose any forces brought into the town by 'the malignant party'.

Few people in fact left the town. They were too afraid that their houses and property might be ransacked and looted by members of the garrison loyal to Goring and the Royalist cause. However some men wisely sent their wives and children out of town. Parliament meanwhile was contemplating what to do for the best. They moved quickly. They sent a messenger to

Portsmouth immediately with instructions for Goring to deliver up the town and to come at once to London himself to answer for his treasonable conduct, and they removed from office his close friend, the governor of the Isle of Wight, the Earl of Portland, who might have been persuaded to provide Goring with supplies and reinforcements. More ominously for Goring, Parliament ordered the Earl of Essex, their military commander, to appoint officers to raise a levy of horse and foot soldiers to proceed to Portsmouth, and if Goring would not hand over the garrison, they were to lay siege to the town.

By early August a sizeable Parliamentary military force had assembled in and around the mainland villages on the slopes of Portsdown hill. It was difficult now not only for Goring to get supplies into the town but also for Royalist sympathisers prepared to fight to get through. By mid-August Sir William Waller had taken charge of the besieging army which was now made up of about 240 horses, troopers and 500 foot soldiers. The Portsmouth garrison contained barely 300 men capable of bearing arms.

The garrison was poorly prepared for a siege. It had barely two days food and there was little prospect of supplies getting in now by either land or sea as a naval squadron was stationed off the coast. The defences were also still in a very poor state despite the large sums of money which had come from both sides in the conflict. According to Clarendon, money which should have been spent on defensive works had been dissipated by Goring in riotous living. His problems were compounded further when the *Henrietta Maria* was taken at night from right beneath his nose by long boats despatched by the naval squadron.

He resolved finally to reduce the scale of defences at Portsbridge and bring ordnance from that site into the town to strengthen the defences there. He also set about requisitioning large quantities of foodstuffs from the local population, to their great distress. According to a contemporary writer, albeit one with parliamentary sympathies, hundreds of cattle, sheep and pigs were driven into the town to be killed and salted down, and their owners' homes were stripped bare of

> *corn, meal, flour, beef, bacon, bread, butter, cheese, eggs, and all their poultry and ducks, not leaving half loaves of bread, nor pieces of bread nor pieces of cheese to the great terror of all the people, especially women and children, forcing poor and rich to come away and beg for bread to keep them alive...*

Seamen from the blockading squadron came to the rescue of some of those afflicted. The men were put ashore on the eastern side of the island with two guns which they used to protect themselves from Goring's men while they engineered the evacuation by sea across Langstone harbour to Hayling Island of a number of women, children and old people. They also took with them about a hundred cattle and two hundred sheep, joined by ropes to the boats and forced to swim.

Parliamentary troops took Portsbridge on the night of 12 August. They were highly elated and one commentator noted that there were 2,000 acres of corn for the taking as whoever held the bridge, in his view, held Portsea Island. They set about strengthening the Portsbridge defences. Two mounts were constructed – and equipped with the guns taken from the *Henrietta Maria*.

A series of skirmishes began now outside the town walls. The morale of local people inside the town was very low. One royalist writer said afterwards that it was necessary not only 'to keep watch over those that were without but those that were within the town,' for many had been pressed into service. By mid-August it was being reported that over half the soldiers and townsmen had quit the town, going over the walls at night. Many of the troops went over to the parliamentary side, 'utterly disliking', it was reported further, 'the colonel's cause and usage of the inhabitants of Portsea Island'.

The blockade by land and sea was a success and work began now on plans to reduce the town – from the Gosport side. Despite the best efforts of Goring's men in the battery on the Portsmouth sea walls, the Gosport men managed to build two

A nineteenth century impression of what the Town Mount must have looked like.
From Gates

Southsea Castle, late sixteenth century, by Alan Sorrell, 1970. The castle had not changed significantly by the mid-seventeenth century. PMRS

gun platforms within a fortnight, one for ten pieces of ordnance and the other for two. Efforts to negotiate peace terms with Goring came to nothing and on Friday 2 September the Gosport gunners opened fire on Portsmouth. They were deadly accurate and terrified Portsmouth's royalist defenders on the Town Mount by the Landport Gate, who spent the night digging trenches into which to fling themselves, if need be, the following day.

The target the next day, Saturday, was the tower of the parish church, which was being used by the defenders as a look-out by land and sea. The gunners

shot through the tower of the church and brake one of the bells, and shot against the tower again, and that rebounded and fell into the church and shot down another top of a house that is near the church, and the end of the church, and shot through a great many houses in the town, but killed not anybody.

The medieval heart of the town was in ruins. As intended, maximum damage was inflicted on key buildings. The onslaught had also distracted Goring from preparations which were underway to take Southsea Castle, which fell to Waller's troops overnight. The garrison at Southsea Castle might have fared better if their commander, Captain Challonor, had not spent Saturday conferring with Goring in Portsmouth and returned 'being something in drink'.

Morale collapsed entirely in the town. The mayor and a number of other leading citizens escaped over the wall. It was clear that the garrison left behind was too small now to mount any effective opposition. Goring surrendered, and the siege ended officially on 7 September. It was an ignominious defeat for Goring but it was for Waller the first of his successes as an army officer on the parliamentary side. The terms negotiated were generous, not least because the garrison had large and very useful supplies of gunpowder in its possession and, if it had chosen to put a match to this stockpile, the town would have been utterly destroyed.

At six o'clock in the evening Goring was rowed out to a ship which would take him to Holland. He reportedly tossed a key into the harbour waters. Some say it was the key to the Square Tower powder magazine, others say it was the key of the town.

CHAPTER 6

Gunfire in the Church
1688

T he Parliamentary side recognised the importance of naval power during the English Civil War. In fact a naval squadron played a key role in the successful blockade of Portsmouth during the siege of the town in August and September 1642. Consequently a great deal of work came to Portsmouth dockyard in the late 1640s and 1650s during the long series of wars, first against the Dutch – the first Dutch War took place 1652–4 – and later, against the French, towards the end of the century.

A new building slip was completed in 1649 and in the 1650s, a new double dry dock was built with a mast wharf, tar house and rope yard. Expansion continued after the Restoration and during the second and third Dutch Wars of 1665-7 and 1672-4.

The town of Portsmouth, 1681. From Gates

Portsmouth harbour and dockyard with the Ropehouse, 1681. From Gates

A new dry dock was built in 1662 and a huge, thousand-foot-long wooden rope house in 1663. A mast pond was completed in 1666 and, with good supplies of timber nearby in the Forest of Bere, Portsmouth became a leading ship-building yard as well as a ship-repair facility.

The town's fortifications were also improved after the Restoration under the supervision of the king's chief engineer, Sir Bernard de Gomme. A major rebuild took place. The town's defences were pushed out to a second moat and related outworks, and the dockyard itself was enclosed with an earth rampart topped with a wooden palisade, and bastions facing south and east.

If Portsmouth was 'the strongest and best fortified' town in the kingdom in 1642, by 1688 it had one of the most impressive defensive systems in Europe, and one of the largest concentrations of troops outside London. And once again, the town played a key role on the national stage, this time during the weeks between the invasion of the Dutch Prince William of Orange and the flight of the king, James II. The catalyst was a mutiny of local army officers: the affair of the 'Portsmouth Captains'.

While the town had benefited significantly from the prodigious sums spent by the king in the dockyard, on the garrison and the fortifications, this, combined with his increasingly autocratic activities, put the expenditure in an entirely different light. 'Portsmouth,' as Robert Jordan suggests in his study of Portsmouth during the 'Glorious Revolution' of 1688, 'began to take on a sinister appearance to the country at large, at once the bastion of autocracy and the open-doorway to that heartland of arbitrary power, catholic France.'

The real issue was the king's religious policy. As a Roman Catholic, he wanted a Declaration of Indulgence (for those who wished to practise the Catholic faith), and the repeal of the Penal Laws and the Test Act. He claimed to be doing this in the name of liberty of conscience and equality of rights but most of his subjects saw his actions as a plot to subvert Protestantism and our national institutions and hand them over to Roman Catholics. James was impervious to the feelings of his countrymen and pursued his policies tenaciously and, arguably, pig-headedly, against mounting anti-Catholic sentiment.

Such sentiment began to express itself in Portsmouth as early as September 1686, when the size of the garrison was doubled, and as barrack accommodation was limited, many local people were forced, reluctantly, to take the new troops into their own homes. Early in the new year the king tried to secure support for his policies in the country by securing loyal addresses – from groups of individuals, from non-conformist churches and borough corporations. Outraged by the behaviour of the troops on the streets and in their homes, and anxious generally about the king's activities, Portsmouth's mayor and corporation conspicuously refused to send such an address.

Only when the doughty Lord Lieutenant and Governor of Portsmouth, the Earl of Gainsborough, who had bolstered civic resistance, was removed from office at the end of the year and replaced by the king's illegitimate son, the energetic Earl of Berwick, did Portsmouth send an acceptable although somewhat half-hearted address to the king.

Matters came to a head however in 1688. Early in the new year France and Holland began to mobilise. Relations between the king and his son-in-law, William of Orange, whose wife, the Protestant Princess Mary, was James's heir, were strained now to near breaking point. Rumours began circulating of an anti-Dutch coalition with France, and stories of five regiments of French soldiers being posted to this country – to be based in Portsmouth! The birth in June of an infant Prince of Wales to the ageing king and his Italian wife, Queen Mary, increased existing tensions even further. Assuming the child thrived, the succession would pass in due course not to the Protestant Princess Mary, and her husband, William of Orange, but to this new English prince who would have been raised as a Roman Catholic.

It should therefore have been no surprise to the king and his intimates that news began circulating that the Dutch were mobilising, not against France but against England – and that the rumours of French troops on English soil might become a distinct reality very shortly. A force of up to 15,000 Frenchmen was believed to be poised for embarkation. It was believed that they would be landing at Portsmouth, and be charged to defend the town in order to keep lines of communication open with France.

The king in fact declined what offers did come from France but the country was now distinctly alarmed and no more so than in Portsmouth, where the king's efforts to mobilise the fleet proceeded apace, and Portsmouth's already swollen peacetime garrison was now put on a war footing with another two regiments of foot. These new regiments had been brought over by the king from Ireland. They were native Irish and overwhelmingly Catholic. The king's enemies used the situation to their own advantage superbly. They exploited the religious paranoia and racial bigotry which existed in the country at large through rumour and in widely-distributed pamphlets.

The first detachment of troops to arrive in Portsmouth in September had some forty men surplus to requirements. The Earl of Berwick ordered his own regiment, Princess Anne of Denmark's foot, to absorb them into their ranks. It was a provocative step. The garrison, the army at large and the general public had been roused now to a fever-pitch of discontent. Fears of having our traditional enemy camping literally on our doorstep, anger at the numbers of Catholic officers appointed by James quite illegally to positions of high command in the army, and distress caused by the way James had turned a Protestant army in Ireland into a Catholic one, combined now to persuade six company commanders in Portsmouth, and their colonel, to refuse to absorb the surplus Irish troopers into their ranks.

The outraged king ordered their arrest and they were despatched to London under close guard where in due course they appeared before a court martial convened at Windsor Castle. They became national heroes. The trial was reported widely, ballads were composed about the 'Portsmouth captains' celebrating their stand against a tyrannical monarch, and their portraits were engraved and sold. The king tried to defuse the situation by just dismissing them from army service but in Portsmouth events were getting rapidly out of hand.

Word had reached James by September from Holland that an invasion was imminent. Yet more troops were posted to those sea-port towns where landings were likely, and Portsmouth received yet more concentrations of Irish troops. They were billeted on the local population. Ill-disciplined, violent and predatory, the stories of their sojourn in the town are legion.

Afterwards, the mayor reported in the Election Book that the town had been

> *a long time opprest and burthened with the Insolency of an Irish and Popish Garrison who have Committed divers lamentable Murthers and grievous outrages upon us they have made themselves absolute Masters of our houses and goods and by free quartering upon us have utterly impoverishd our Towne and places adjacent and threatned to blow up the magazeene and forts here and utterly to destroy and extirpate us.*

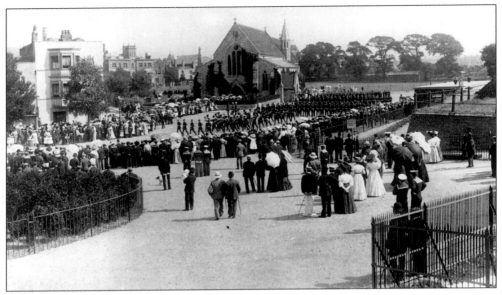

The Garrison Church, c.1900. PMRS

Many families who were able to do so quit the town. The mayor himself was actually attacked and robbed at night by 'the rude Irish' as he went about his business. A brawl took place in early October when a group of Irish soldiers broke into an alehouse looking for drink and, being taken to task by some Englishmen, set upon them and beat off 'two files of English musketeers, in which quarrel its said four or five were killed and several wounded, and that two officers are run through the body'. More typical was the allegation made later in the month at the Borough Sessions by a soldier called John Collins that 'last night lodging at the house of Margaret Bee he had and paid for a flagon of beer and would have had another, but she refused and said the Duke was a rogue and the King was a fool for sending such fellows thither'.

The worst incident took place at the end of October as well. A 'great disorder' took place between

Souldiers of the Duke of Berwicks Regiment and the Irish Regiment commanded by Coll Mackillicut which tis said was Occasion'd by an Irish Souldier firing into the Church with Bullet in time of divine Service – the present account is that 50 or 60 are killed and wounded on both Sides.

St Thomas's Church, *c.* 1900. PMRS

The details of what exactly took place vary from one report to another. Elsewhere it was reported that some forty were killed on the spot, that a number of Irishmen had fired into the church, and that twenty-two of them were in prison in the town awaiting trial. The church in question must have been the Garrison Church, the chapel of the old Domus Dei, now part of the Governor's complex of buildings alongside the parade ground. It had been in use as the parish church since St Thomas's was almost destroyed in the siege of 1642. Burial records of the Garrison Church and St Thomas's do not appear to have survived for this period, so we have no formal record of the names of those who died in this particular incident. The only burial which may be connected with what happened is that of Edward Slingsby, 'the sonn of Major Slingsby of Portsmouth', who was buried in the churchyard of St Mary's Portsea on 19 October.

The most recent influx of Irish troops was also accompanied by some significant changes at Government House. Edward Slingsby's father, Henry Slingsby, a former Lieutenant Governor and the Town Major, was replaced by two of the king's men. The new Lieutenant Governor appointed, Sir Edward Scott, was a particularly violent man. Those local citizens who had not moved out watched these developments, and listened to rumours of the despatch of yet more troops to Portsmouth, with increasing alarm. The diarist, John Evelyn, actually recorded that the king 'continues to remove Protestants and put papists into Portsmouth and other places of trust'.

It all seemed to give credence to other rumours that Queen Mary and the baby Prince of Wales were about to leave London and take up residence near Portsmouth. If need be, they could seek protection within the walls of the fortress and, if the worst came to the worst, they would be well placed to arrange their passage out of the country. Other plausible rumours had it that the king planned to arrest his enemies and imprison them, not in the Tower of London but at Portsmouth. The town was in turmoil.

The Prince of Wales was brought to Portsmouth, and lodged in Alderman Ridge's house in the High Street. He stayed there only briefly though for by this time the Dutch invasion force had put to sea and was heading down the English Channel along the south coast. It was feared that Portsmouth might well find itself on the front line.

In fact the Dutch sailed on and William of Orange landed at Tor Bay. From there he set off for London. There was open fighting now on the streets of Portsmouth between different groups of soldiers and sailors. Support for the king from the fleet and its commander, Lord Dartmouth, evaporated fast. Threatened by royal officials to press local men to work on strengthening the town's defences, the mayor and other prominent local citizens fled to the relative safety of Dartmouth's flagship.

James now sent Berwick, who was, after all, titular governor of Portsmouth, to take personal command of the town but before Berwick arrived, James fled the country, though not in fact through Portsmouth. Matters had gone from bad to worse there. There were hundreds of disaffected troops, many from the much-feared Irish regiments, and dismissed now from army service, roaming the streets of the town and the surrounding countryside in marauding packs. The situation was saved by the redoubtable old Civil War veteran, Colonel Richard Norton of Southwick, who raised a strong local force of foot soldiers and horsemen and effectively blockaded Portsea Island. Relief for the town came finally just before Christmas 1688, when the new garrison of Prince William's men arrived and later, sufficient barracks were built to accommodate the local garrison, thus relieving the aggrieved local population from a much hated imposition.

Early in the new year Colonel Norton – the hero of the hour – and Henry Slingsby were returned as MPs for the borough. The Election Book records that this would be

a Free Parliament for the preservation of the Protestant Religion, and restoring the rights and liberties of the Kingdome and settling the same that they may not be in danger againe of being subverted.

CHAPTER 7

The Spithead Mutiny
1797

n 17 April 1797, on board *Monarch* in Portsmouth Harbour, a young naval officer, Lieutenant Beaver, wrote to his sister, Mrs Gillies – Kate – of Portman Street, Portman Square, London:

You have doubtless heard of the situation of the Fleet at Spithead. They have, every ship, refused to go to Sea 'till that pay is increased, unless the French Fleet should be out in which case they are ready and willing to go.

As an officer, he concluded, he condemned such conduct, and the timing was hardly ideal but

as *a man I can find many excuses for them – I could say many things to extenuate their conduct and I cannot but admire their moderation in so daring an exercise of illegal power – and their patriotism.*

He was not alone in his sympathy for the men. Pay or, rather, the lack of it, for it had not been increased since the time of Charles II, poor food, impressment, savage discipline and, in case the men deserted, little or no shore leave had created simmering discontent below decks.

The Admiralty was first warned that a general mutiny was possible as early as 1795, by the transport officer at Portsmouth. He was responsible for bringing the newly-pressed men to join their ships. 1795 was also the year that two new pieces of legislation were passed to recruit additional, desperately-needed, men for the navy but which, unwittingly, contributed to the developing crisis. The first required each county to raise a number of men roughly proportional to their population. The second required each port to supply a quota of recruits. The magistrates fulfilled their obligations by emptying the gaols of

'Portsmouth Point' by Thomas Rowlandson, c. 1800. PMRS

minor criminals such as thieves, pickpockets, beggars and poachers. They also offered bounties to those who volunteered for naval service. These new recruits – quota men - tended to be better educated than the average seamen. Some were failed business men or former school teachers who were attracted by the bounties. They had organizational skills and between them, had some knowledge of the democratic ideas beginning to circulate, which deplored the inhumane treatment of one section of humanity by another. Confronted by the appalling conditions they discovered below decks some of these new recruits set about mobilising resistance to the status quo.

The man who led the campaign in Portsmouth was called Valentine Joyce, a twenty-six-year-old quartermaster's mate. He was alleged to be a 'quota' man but his parents lived in Portsmouth and had done so for many years. His father was a former soldier and still served in the garrison invalid corps, which was made up of old and partially disabled soldiers still fit enough for garrison duty. Whatever his career history, Joyce and his fellow-plotters pulled off a major planning feat. Using the relative freedom given the men to visit each other's ships on Sunday afternoons, they made their plans undetected.

A single petition was drawn up concentrating solely on the issue of pay. It was circulated to be copied by each ship and in due course eleven letters were smuggled ashore and sent to Lord Howe who, they hoped, would send them on to the Lord Commissioners of the Admiralty. Lord Howe was the hero of the Glorious First of June, the first great sea battle between the British and French fleets in the French Revolutionary War, which was fought some three hundred miles off the coast of Brittany in 1794. He was very popular with the lower decks but he was seventy-one now, retired, and living in Bath where he was severely incapacitated with gout.

He said of the letters later in the House of Lords:

> *They were all exact copies of each other, limited solely to a request for an increase of pay, that the seamen might be able to make better provision for their families, decently expressed, but without any signature. I could not reply to applications which were anonymous, nor acknowledge the receipt of them to parties unavowed and unascertained. About four or five of the petitions first received, though little different in the handwriting, were obviously dictated by the same person, and I had therein further reason to think they were fabricated by some malicious individual, who meant to insinuate the prevalence of a general discontent in the fleet.*

However, he did send the letters to an officer in Portsmouth, asking him whether he was aware of any dissatisfaction in the fleet. The reply was no. Clearly still somewhat disturbed by their content, he took the letters to London when he had recovered sufficiently from the gout, and showed them to Lord Spencer, the First Lord of the Admiralty. Lord Spencer's reaction was predictable. Ultimately only Parliament could sanction any increase in seamen's pay, and he was reluctant to apply for more money when taxes had already reached punitive levels and the government was urging financial stringency. Consequently he did nothing.

The men had waited a whole month for a government response. They could only conclude that Lord Howe had let them down. They resolved now to petition parliament directly, and when they returned from the forthcoming cruise under the command of Lord Bridport, Commander of the Channel Fleet,

The First Semaphore. From Gates

they would refuse to go to sea again until their demands were met

By now lower-deck informers were reporting that grievance meetings were taking place daily, and that correspondence was passing freely from ship to ship. Astonishingly, Lord Bridport made no effort to investigate these reports. Finally, on 12 April, one of his captains, Captain Patton, on a trip out to the *Queen Charlotte* at Spithead, was sufficiently alarmed by what he saw to send a message to the Admiralty when he returned to shore by the newly-installed telegraph or semaphore on Southsea Beach. Within a few minutes the message was received on the Admiralty roof, 'Mutiny brewing at Spithead.'

Lord Bridport himself now awoke finally to the reality of the drama unfolding round him. He sent an express despatch to London the following day, informing the Admiralty that

The Mutineers' Petition to Parliament, 18 April, 1797. PMRS 1270A/5/1.

TO

The Right Honourable and the Honourable Knights, Citizens and Burgesses in Parliament assembled.

THE

HUMBLE PETITION

Of the SEAMEN and MARINES on Board His Majesty's Ships, in behalf of themselves,

HUMBLY SHEWETH,

THAT your Petitioners relying on the Candour and Justice of your Honourable House, make bold to lay their Grievances before you, hoping, that when you reflect on them, you will please to give Redress, as far as your Wisdom shall deem necessary.

We beg Leave to remind your august Assembly, that the Act of Parliament passed in the Reign of

'disagreeable combinations' were forming on board the ships. Sensibly, he also summoned his captains, asked them to muster their men and urge them to set out their grievances fully and specifically in a new set of petitions. To his astonishment, the Admiralty's response to his recent despatch was to order him to put to sea on 16 April, and to send his subordinate, Sir Alan Gardner, ahead of him with eight ships to the St Helen's anchorage, which was the usual starting-point for a cruise. He told the Admiralty that he doubted very much whether these orders would be obeyed and indeed, when Sir Alan tried to carry out his instructions to sail, he was met with an adamant refusal.

Boats from the *Queen Charlotte* and *Royal George* now visited each ship, telling the men to stand firm. Valentine Joyce told them to allow their officers to stay on board, and to obey all orders other than those to sail. Each crew was also charged to send two men to a committee meeting that evening on board *Queen Charlotte*.

Lieutenant Beaver on board the *Monarch* added a postscript to his letter to Kate of 17 April. The situation was now 'very serious,' he wrote, and using vocabulary ominously reminiscent of revolutionary France, he reported that a convention of deputies from each ship was now meeting daily on board *Queen Charlotte*.

Lord Bridport sent the new petitions and an account of developments post haste to the Admiralty. He recommended that their lordships should comply in some measure with the prayers of the petitioners. They would not, and reiterated their message to him to put to sea. The men refused to do so once again.

The committee which met regularly on the *Queen Charlotte*– the central committee – was made up of two delegates from sixteen line-of-battle ships – the eight at St Helen's and the other eight at Spithead. Interestingly the committee confined the mutiny in due course to these ships only. Frigates and sloops, they judged, had important work to do which should not be left undone, and they defended themselves stoutly from charges of treason, infidelity and treachery. A satirical pamphlet was published by Admiral Kempenfeldt's ghost severely criticising their behaviour, to which they responded:

If the Clamours of Justice, daily echoing from the Mouths of the LOYAL TARS, should again awake the SPIRIT OF

From *the* LIVING *to the* DEAD.

" *Art thou a Spirit of Earth, or Goblin damn'd.*"

SIR,

IN the Sun of the 18th Inftant, we have feen your Addrefs, and which greatly furprized us, wherein we are accufed of thofe Crimes which difgrace the Name of a Britifh Seaman, and which may prejudice the Minds of our Countrymen againft us; as we are called upon to make known our Wants and Wifhes in an official and refpeâful Manner.

Therefore we, His Majefty's moft Loyal Subjeâs, wifh to make known to the World that we have done fo.

We, as the Subjeâs of a Loyal Country, prefented our Petition to that Honorable EARL who wore the Laurels of the Glorious FIRST OF JUNE, and who was in the Hearts of Britifh Seamen reprefented as their Friend, but forry are we to fay that we found to the Contrary, in his not reprefenting our Petitions to the Lords Commiffioners of the Admiralty.

But to convince our Country at large, that there is not in anywife the leaft Spark of Republican Spirit, we have caufed to be inferted the moft private of our Concerns; forry alfo we are to remark the Words *(French Agents)* as our Country may think, by that Affertion, we now take into our Arms the People that a Britifh Seaman detefts the Name of. But to the contrary, we have our Country's Good as much at Heart as any other Defcription of Men whatever, and that our Requeft is nowife injurious to our Country.

We afk for that comfortable Subfiftence which our Country can eafily beftow, and that thofe Barbarities which are praâifed by fome, (forry indeed we fhould be to fay the whole, as there are among us Men of every Defcription, both good and evil) be erafed out of this well-inftituted Service.

We, the Subjeâs of your Addrefs, coolly as the Reprefentatives of that Body which has fo long lain under the well-known Buoy, wifh you to come forward in a fair and manly way, in your real and corporeal State, and try for one Week if the fcanty Allowance on which we are obliged to fubfift, will keep you in the fpirited State which Men of our Defcription require, but are at this Moment without the Affiftance of at leaft Two-thirds of their Pay; and our Wives and Families languifhing in Want, whilft this Country that abounds with Plenty, ought to be afhamed at the word **Want.**

To the Brave Admiral Kempenfeldt's GHOST,
Buoy of the Royal George, Spithead.

P. S. If the Clamours of Juftice, daily echoing from the Mouths of the LOYAL TARS, fhould again awake the SPIRIT of KEMPENFELDT, let not his ethereal but his corporeal Part make itfelf known, and we will convince him, that thofe who have made *Britannia Rule the Main,* know alfo their Duty to their Sovereign.

SPITHEAD, *April* 20, 1797.

Squib: Admiral Kempenfeldt's Ghost, 20 April, 1797. PMRS 1270A/5/3.

KEMPENFELDT, let not his ethereal but his corporeal Part make itself known, and we will convince him, that those who have made Britannia Rule the Main know also their Duty to their Sovereign.

They reminded readers that they asked

for that comfortable Subsistence which our Country can easily bestow, and that those Barbarities which are practised by some, (sorry indeed we should be to say the whole, as there are among us Men of every Description, both good and evil) be erased out of this well-instituted Service.

Another squib, as these documents were called, dwelt on the plight of the widow of a seaman 'Who lost his Life in the Defence of his Country, on board the INTREPID, in the present War':

The Genius of Britain went hovering round,
For she fear'd that fair Freedom was fled,
But she found to her Joy that she was not quite gone
But remain'd with the Fleet at Spithead.

Rejoic'd at the News to the Charlotte she flew,
Where fair Freedom she heard sat enthron'd;
They all mann'd the Yards as the Goddess came in,
For Britain and Freedom they own'd.

The Fleet hail'd the Goddess with three hearty Cheers,
As she stood on the Charlotte's Gangway;
She dropp'd a sad tear as she look'd on her Sons,
Who so long neglected had lay.

And thus the piece continued for another five verses, underscoring the validity of their cause and their loyalty to king and country. They were responsible men. The country was at war. The delegates themselves were in fact widely respected. Lord Bridport himself said so afterwards. He called them 'the best men aboard', 'the good and leading men' and 'the best behaved and reliable'. There were petty officers and at least five midshipmen of mature years in their ranks.

The delegates now called on the seamen to swear an oath to be true to their cause. This was to bring everyone into line including

LINES,

(Compofed on Board His Majefty's Ship LONDON)

BY

The WIDOW of a SEAMAN,

Who loft his Life in the Defence of his Country, on Board the INTREPID, in the prefent War.

THE Genius of Britain went hovering round,
  For fhe fear'd that fair Freedom was fled,
But fhe found to her Joy that fhe was not quite gone,
  But remain'd with the Fleet at Spithead.

Rejoic'd at the News to the *Charlotte* fhe flew,
  Where fair Freedom fhe heard fat enthron'd ;
They all mann'd the Yards as the Goddefs came in,
  For Britain and Freedom they own'd

The Fleet hail'd the Goddefs with three hearty Cheers,
  As fhe ftood on the *Charlotte's* Gangway ;
She dropp'd a fad Tear as fhe look'd on her Sons,
  Who fo long neglected had lay.

She was led to the Cabin, fair Freedom was there,
  True Loyalty fat by her Side,
BRITANNIA fat down in a Tranfport of Joy,
  All hail to my Heroes, fhe cry'd.

Every Ship of the Line fent two Seamen fo brave,
  Whom the Goddefs receiv'd with a Smile ;
They affur'd her that if they were treated like Men,
  They would ftill guard her favourite Ifle.

Go on my brave Sons in the Steps you now tread,
  Be Virtue your Guide and your Guard ;
And GOD, who rules over the Land and Sea,
  Will your honeft Endeavours reward.

The Genius of *Ireland* came in with her Harp,
  She faluted fair Freedom with Tears :
They all mann'd the Yards to welcome her o'er
  And ev'ry Ship gave her three Cheers.

Succefs to the Seventeen united bright Stars,
  Let their praife echo round ev'ry Shore,
And the 15th of April will ne'er be forgot,
  Till Britain and Freedom 're no more.

Squib: Lines by the Widow of a Seaman, April, 1797. PMRS 1270A/5/5.

any possible waverers, fearful perhaps of the consequences of their actions. Most of the petty officers and marines sympathised strongly with the seamen's plight and took the oath too, despite the fact that the latter were on board ship to police the seamen.

As well as the delegates' committee, each ship had a lower deck committee and events seemed now to take a sinister turn. The men began to hang ropes from the yardarms. Their intention was to instil order amongst their fellow crew members. Certainly this was what Lieutenant Beaver understood. They have done it, he wrote, 'more with a view towards preventing any of their own party seceding than with an intention of intimidating the officers'. It was not how it appeared to the onlookers on shore though where this new development was interpreted as just that - an effort to intimidate the officers on board.

At long last Lord Spencer stirred himself and decided on 17 April that he had better come down to Portsmouth with two of his colleagues. Lord Bridport passed on the news to the ships at once. They were delighted – and set about at once preparing a longer list of demands which extended now to food, leave and better treatment for the sick and wounded. They persisted that they were asking for nothing 'but what is Moderate, and may be granted without detriment to the Nation or Injury to the Service'.

Lord Spencer and his party travelled overnight to Portsmouth and ensconced themselves the following morning in the *Fountain*, the grandest of the inns in the High Street. There they summoned Lord Bridport to appear before them. When he arrived he presented them with the latest petition. They refused to consider it and insisted on confining their attention to the original issue of pay. They offered increases from 22s. to 26s. 6d. a month for petty officers and able seamen, and from 19s. to 22s. for ordinary seamen, and created a new category of landsman at 21s. a month. The offer was declined. After due debate, the committee asked for another 1s. 6d a month for all ratings and marines on top of the original offer, refused to recognise the new category of landsman and returned to their demand for better rations. They would not put to sea until their grievances were redressed and an act of indemnity – a pardon - obtained.

The men, wrote Lieutenant Beaver, 'have demanded nothing but what to every unprejudiced person must appear moderate and just'. After two days of negotiations, he added, 'the Admiralty have been sitting…at Portsmouth without having finally resolved to do what will and must be forced from them – how much better had they at once come handsomely into the proposals.'

The Admiralty did agree finally to pay the increase demanded but retained the category of landsman. They also refused to discuss rations, shore leave or other grievances. The proposal on pay was in fact received favourably but all agreed to wait, and see what the committee of delegates on board *Queen Charlotte* agreed to recommend. But as the representatives of *Royal Sovereign*, Sir Alan Gardner's flagship, rowed away to the meeting of delegates on board *Queen Charlotte*, Sir Alan decided to take matters into his own hands, and see what he could do to speed up the negotiations. He decided that he would go over to *Queen Charlotte* himself, accompanied by Admiral Colpoys and other officers and address the delegates himself. When he arrived the meeting of delegates had not in fact begun, because Valentine Joyce and several others of the committee had been detained by business on shore. Sir Alan seized this opportunity to try and talk the men round. Rashly he invoked Lord Spencer's statement in a recent note that

> *if the men…do not immediately accede to the terms offered they may rely on it (they being all well known) that they will be brought to condign punishment and suffer the utmost vengeance of the law. But, on the contrary, should they submit with alacrity, they will experience the forgiveness for which the Board of Admiralty have publicly and solemnly pledged their faith to them.*

The sentiment of the meeting seemed to swing in Sir Alan's favour but at this point Joyce and his companions returned, and they insisted that unless there was a direct pardon for them all from the king himself, there could be no return to duty. The meeting veered now in this direction. Sir Alan lost his temper. He accused Joyce and his fellow-delegates of being 'a mutinous blackguard set that deserves hanging' and with his companions, he was hustled unceremoniously off the ship.

Joyce decided now to call another meeting, this time on his ship, *Royal George*. A pre-arranged signal was hoisted, a red flag. Red flags were normally flown only when a ship was going into action, and the officers on board and watchers on shore interpreted this signal as meaning bloody revolution, particularly as the delegates, after Sir Alan's outburst and departure, had ordered the guns to be mounted, the fleet prepared for action and the officers to be confined below.

Lord Spencer was persuaded finally that the only way to secure the men's return to duty was to obtain the royal pardon. He set off back to London. The pardon was quickly obtained from the king at Windsor. One hundred copies were printed rapidly in London, despatched overnight to Portsmouth and distributed the following morning to the different ships' companies. Lord Bridport himself read the proclamation of pardon on his own ship – and made a speech promising a general redress of grievances. His crew cheered, the ropes were taken down from the yardarms and his own flag was hoisted in place of the red flag. One by one the other ships followed suit.

As the different ships' boats came ashore that evening, word that the men's demands had been met, and a proclamation of pardon obtained, spread quickly. There was a great deal of sympathy in Portsmouth for the seamen and their cause and the good news 'was received with the most excessive joy by the people on shore'. The local magistrates were pleased too, for the long years of war had brought many of the wives and children of seamen to the town. With little or no money many had become dependent on the parish poor rates.

Lord Bridport now felt confident enough to take six ships down to St Helen's to await orders to sail. His best efforts to restore order were thrown into complete confusion however when he received the Admiralty's reply to the seamen's fuller demands of a few day's earlier. The Admiralty discounted entirely the complaints about food, declined to increase pensions at Greenwich Hospital and said that no officer complained of would be removed without application through proper channels for courts-martial. Lord Bridport suppressed the document but he could do nothing about Lord Spencer's dilatoriness in notifying the Privy Council of the proposed pay increases which had been agreed. This was singularly unfortunate as it was the Privy Council which initiated the money bills for Parliament.

In their innocence, the seamen thought that a few days would be sufficient for their pay agreement to be given the force of law, and they became increasingly convinced that they had been tricked. On top of their growing suspicions, came the crass ill-timing of a document sent out now by the Admiralty to the captains of all ships, instructing them to tighten up on discipline, see that the marines' arms and ammunition were in good order and ready for use, and to 'be ready on the first appearance of mutiny to use the most vigorous means to suppress it'. The captains, sensibly, kept very quiet about these orders but the men became suspicious when they saw the marines' stores and equipment being checked over. Their anxieties were fuelled further when they heard of the question asked in the House of Lords as to whether ministers had any comments to make on recent events in the Navy – and Lord Spencer said he had no comment to make.

The seamen were now convinced that they had been double-crossed. On the day before Parliament was in fact due to debate the bill to increase seamen's pay the wind changed and in theory it was now possible for Lord Bridport to put to sea. However he knew that they would refuse to sail unless they received confirmation that their money was on its way. He declined to give the order to sail but, notwithstanding this decision, the men had had enough. The second Spithead mutiny broke out now.

A pre-arranged outburst of cheering rang out from each ship at St Helen's, ropes reappeared at yard arms and red flags were run up. Boats went from ship to ship encouraging the crews. Delegates now resolved to take a procession of boats to Spithead to persuade the crews of the ships of the line anchored there to bring their ships down to St Helen's, out of range of the powerful Portsmouth shore batteries.

At the Spithead anchorage Sir John Colpoys, on board *London* and possibly still smarting from his undignified exit from *Queen Charlotte,* determined to resist such insubordination. He mustered his crew and read the Articles of War. At this point some confusion arose between the men and Sir John. Sir John concluded, erroneously, that the men were now satisfied that their demands had been met, and he ordered them to be confined below although a few still lingered on deck forward. He also ordered the lower-deck guns to be run in and the port-lids to be closed, to prevent communication with the boats approaching from St Helen's. Officers, with men Sir John trusted, were posted to guard the hatches and entries, and to stay with him to confront those lingering on the forecastle.

The procession from St Helen's pulled up alongside the *Marlborough* first. The unpopular captain offered no resistance and he was put ashore with other officers who were equally disliked. The ship was then taken down to St Helen's. Meanwhile, on board *London*, events began to unravel. The men confined below deck began to push up the hatchways. On Sir John's instructions, the officers opened fire, which was returned by some seamen. A number on both sides fell wounded, three seamen fatally.

Sir John ordered the marines forward but only two –
foreigners – obeyed their officers' orders. The rest threw down
their arms and went over to the mutineers. It was madness to
resist further. Sir John ordered his men to cease firing and
retreated to the poop with his officers. In the succeeding melee
the young first lieutenant of *London*, Peter Bover, was seized. He
had shot down a man on the forecastle trying to unlash a gun
and turn it on the quarterdeck. A noose was placed over his
neck but his life was saved by the unlikely combination of
Valentine Joyce and Sir John Colpoys. Joyce had served under
Bover in another ship, and he fought his way through the crowd
shouting that if they hanged Bover, they could hang him too,
and Sir John roared out that Bover was only obeying his orders.
He added further that he was only obeying orders too – and
produced the Admiralty's orders of a few days before, ordering
captains to be ready on the first appearance of mutiny to use
their utmost means to suppress such activities. The document
was seized and he and two of his senior officers were taken
below – to be tried by a lower-deck court.

Officers on the other ships at Spithead were put ashore now
with the exception of the three prisoners on board *London*.
Those injured in the action on *London* had their wounds dressed
and were then taken ashore to Haslar Hospital. There three of
the badly wounded died. The seamen wished to take them in
procession to be buried in the churchyard of St Mary's Portsea
at Kingston but the military authorities would not sanction a
procession of seamen through the town of Portsmouth, which
had been put now on a war footing. The fortifications had been
manned by the resident garrison, the drawbridges had been
raised and the guns prepared for action. There was real fear of
a clash between the seamen and the garrison. Fortunately
commonsense prevailed in the person of the mayor, Sir John
Carter, who negotiated with the seamen a route which involved
them bringing the coffins by boat from Gosport to the Hard in
London's barge and carrying them, with a procession of some
fifty of their former colleagues following behind, through the
streets of Portsea and across the fields to Kingston.

The delegates of the *London* wrote gratefully to Sir John
Carter afterwards, thanking him for his sympathetic understanding:

The very distinguished manner in which you was pleased to
treat the part of our Ship's Company which were on Shore

Yesterday attending the Funeral of our Unfortunate Shipmates yesterday claims the attention of every heart endued with the smallest Spark of Humanity.

The government now at last moved smartly to push through the legislation necessary to secure the increases in pay promised the seamen, and sought the assistance of Lord Howe in taking the news of the bill's successful passage through Parliament to Portsmouth. So, accompanied by Lady Howe, and travelling overnight through fierce wind and rain, Lord Howe arrived finally in Portsmouth on the morning of 10 May.

For three whole days he moved from one ship to the next, speaking with the men, explaining what had been agreed and hearing them out. In that time he also arranged for Sir John Colpoys and the other officers confined on board *London* with him, to be handed over to the civil authorities. A document survives in the City Records Office made out to the ship's company of the *London* and signed by Sir John Carter certifying that Vice Admiral John Colpoys, Captain Edward Griffiths, Lieutenant Randal McDonald, Edward Hoare and Mr William FitzWilliam Ower had been delivered into the hands of the civic power and were now in the writer's custody.

On the fourth day Lord Howe met with the delegates on board *Royal William* to discuss the removal of unpopular officers. He agreed finally to recommend to the Admiralty that some fifty-nine officers (half of those put ashore) should be superseded. Aside from the issue of shore leave, the men's demands had been met.

Lord Howe was utterly exhausted by this time but his work was not yet quite done. He had to enter the fray once more when the Western Squadron arrived at this moment at Spithead from Plymouth, flying the red flag and with its officers confined below decks. He went aboard the flagship and, in return for him agreeing to remove another tranche of officers, the Western Squadron in turn now agreed to haul down the red flags.

Lord Howe was finally escorted ashore by a flotilla of small boats and was received by rapturous crowds at Point. He walked from there to Government House with Lady Howe on his arm. Valentine Joyce was in the crowd there. He stepped forward to make arrangements with Lord Howe about the timings for the formal celebrations the following day. Lord Howe invited him into Government House to take a glass of wine. It was a very civilised end to hostilities. The pardon arrived the following day.

CHAPTER 8

The Last Fatal Duel in England
1845

T he development of recreational facilities in the late eighteenth century, overlooking the sea and to the east of the fortifications, where both local residents and visitors could meet their friends, take the air or soak in hot baths, launched Portsmouth or rather, Southsea, its new middle-class suburb, as a watering place and fashionable resort.

The first rather insubstantial wooden structures were replaced in 1817 by a much more robust building which became a fashionable social centre particularly for local naval and military families. It was purchased in 1821 by Henry Hollingsworth. He spent a considerable amount of money on improving the facilities and by the late 1820s there were not only suites of baths but a library, and an assembly room where balls and other social events took place. The complex was named the King's Rooms in 1830, in honour of William IV who succeeded his brother as king that year, and had been associated with the town since his days as a midshipman. It remained the

King's Rooms and view across the Little Morrass towards Old Portsmouth, early nineteenth century. From Gates

town's most fashionable meeting-place for many years and it was there, in 1845, that insults traded between two officers on the dance floor led to what is claimed was the last fatal duel in England – fought over a lady.

Duelling was almost a local pastime at this period due to the large numbers of naval and military men stationed in the town and its environs. Appeals to arms in vindication of outraged honour were numerous. A duel took place on 6 November 1800 in a passage behind the *Blue Posts* in Broad Street, between Lieutenant Stapleton of the 20th Foot and Ensign Grainger of the Guards, following a quarrel over the question of precedence in the Army. Stapleton's pistol missed fire and Grainger's ball went wide. Stapleton insisted upon his right to a shot and, aiming deliberately, shot Grainger in the thigh. He died from the wound some four days later and was buried in the grounds of the Garrison Church. Stapleton was arrested and tried in due course at the Assizes in Winchester. He was found guilty of manslaughter, sentenced to six months imprisonment and fined £50, but this was mitigated and he was in fact released from prison having served barely nine weeks of his sentence.

Another duel took place a few months later in April 1801 at Fort Monckton between two young officers of the West Norfolk Regiment, one of whom was so severely wounded that he died the same evening. A dispute between two naval officers, Lieutenant Charlton of HMS *Mars* and Lieutenant Guthrie of the Royal Marines, took place in July 1807. One accused the other of lying. Pistols were drawn at twelve paces. Lieutenant Charlton was hit in the thigh and died subsequently in Haslar Hospital. A verdict of wilful murder was returned by the coroner's jury but Lieutenant Charlton was acquitted at the Assizes.

Another argument, this time between two Royal Marines officers, Lieutenant Bagnall and Lieutenant Stuart, culminated in pistols on Southsea Common in October 1812, and the following year a duel took place between Lieutenant John Blundell of the 101st Regiment and Ensign Edward Macguire of the 6th West India Regiment at Carisbrooke on the Isle of Wight. At the second discharge Blundell received a mortal wound and died two days later. Macguire was found guilty in due course and sentenced to death but was pardoned eventually. He seems to have been the unwitting tool of others, and particularly of one Lieutenant Dillon who had been jilted by Blundell's wife, reputedly a great beauty and the daughter of

Mr Henry White, the mayor of Portsmouth, who was knighted by the Prince Regent in 1814 on the occasion of the visit of the allied sovereigns to Portsmouth that year. Mrs Blundell was a remarkable woman. Her first husband was also a military officer. He was ordered abroad however directly after the wedding, and killed in action. Her second husband was Blundell. Before she was nineteen she had had three husbands, and by her fourth, had thirteen children!

The duel – purportedly the last fought in England - which took place at Browndown on 20 May 1845 between Lieutenant Charles Hawkey of the Royal Navy and Captain Alexander Seton of the 11th Dragoons was occasioned by attentions, not altogether unwelcome, paid by Captain Seton to Mrs Hawkey. According to newspaper reports, Seton was 'young, rich and good looking'. He met Mrs Hawkey at the King's Rooms. She was described as 'a most fascinating person' and, although he had a wife of his own, he paid her 'marked attention'.

The developing drama and its tragic denouement can be pieced together from the words of the witnesses called to give evidence, first at the coroner's court which met in the new Guildhall in the High Street, Portsmouth, and subsequently at the Assizes in Winchester. What they had to say was published in meticulous detail in both local and national newspapers, and in *The Illustrated London News* there are even illustrations of the courtroom scene in Winchester. The duel created a sensation throughout the country and the public were avid for detail.

Mrs Hawkey's evidence was followed closely. She told the coroner's court that she met Seton for the first time in Spring 1844 when she was introduced to him by her husband. She danced with him and he asked her to call on Mrs Seton. He was clearly keen to further their acquaintanceship and left presents at her house, including a music book. A number of visits also took place between them. On some occasions Mrs Seton was present when they met at the Setons' residence but there were times when she was not, and there were occasions when her own husband was not present in their lodgings when Seton called there. There were servants present however.

She recalled a soiree at the assembly rooms when Seton gave her a bouquet of flowers. Her husband had not been happy and he intercepted the bouquet and thanked Seton for it. Seton had also said to her that he knew that Hawkey was quarrelsome, and that the whole business was likely to finish with him, Seton, having 'to go out with Mr Hawkey'. Later, he expressed his feelings for her 'forcibly' when his wife was away in London.

Matters soon came to a head. At an assembly at the King's Rooms, Hawkey said that he disliked seeing her with Mr and Mrs Seton. However she did not think that he was fully aware of Seton's attentions to her until the Sunday before the duel in fact took place. She had not informed him of the persecution to which she was being subjected as she was afraid that 'something serious' might take place.

At a subsequent event at the King's Rooms, Seton placed himself in a seat beside her and refused to move when Hawkey wished to sit down by his wife. Hawkey asked to have a private word with him. He reportedly threatened to horsewhip Seton down the High Street unless he was given satisfaction.

Mr Hollingsworth, the proprietor of the King's Rooms, confirmed at the Assizes that at the soiree held at his rooms on 19 May the previous year Hawkey, Seton, Lieutenant Pym (who would serve subsequently as Lieutenant Hawkey's second), and several ladies, attended. They had been subscribers to his rooms for some two to three weeks. One of his stewards reported that he heard Hawkey say 'that Seton is a blackguard and a scoundrel' Another witness who was also within earshot that evening said that he heard Hawkey say that he would shoot Seton 'as he would a partridge'. There was a sensation in court as these words were heard.

Provoked beyond measure, Hawkey clearly called Seton out. On the morning of the duel it was reported that he went to Mr Fisk's in Portsmouth and purchased pistols. He then went to Mr Sherwood's shooting gallery where he ordered bullets to be cast, and asked for some shots. He practised there, and then, according to the evidence of Lieutenant Pym's servant, William Marshall, Hawkey and Lieutenant Pym, with him, William Marshall, crossed the water to Gosport and the relative privacy of Stokes Bay.

William Marshall was told to remain on the shore. Roughly three-quarters of an hour later, he said, Lieutenant Pym came running towards him beckoning. He followed him to a spot where he saw a wounded man lying on the ground, 'bleeding very much'. He was sent to find a doctor. The wounded man was Mr Seton. A later witness confirmed that on the evening in question he heard two reports of a pistol and believed that William Marshall was the man who approached him asking the whereabouts of a doctor.

Seton had apparently been hit with Hawkey's second shot. Hawkey fled and Seton was brought back in due course to Portsmouth. He was lodged at the Quebec Hotel on Point where he subsequently died despite the best efforts of his medical advisers. The cause of death, the coroner's jury found, was

the result of a surgical operation, rendered imperatively necessary by the imminent danger in which he was placed by the infliction of a gun-shot wound he received on 20 May last in a duel between Henry Charles Moorehead Hawkey of the Royal Marines.

The jury found Hawkey and Lieutenant Pym, 'as well as all the parties concerned in the said duel, guilty of wilful murder'. The coroner had acknowledged in his summing up that evidence 'had been given there that day with the view of proving great provocation on the part of Mr Seton, by his having used offensive words'. 'That might have been', he said, 'but it did not alter the features of the case'. 'All persons', he said

who, according to any preconcerted arrangement, go out for the purpose of fighting with deadly weapons after a quarrel, however grievous it might have been, are guilty of wilful murder.

He issued a warrant for their trial at the assizes in Winchester. However, there, with the help of powerful counsel in the person of Mr Cockburn, later Lord Chief Justice Cockburn, and a jury sympathetic to Hawkey's plea that he had received much provocation, a verdict of not guilty was returned.

HANGED IN CHAINS

CHAPTER 9

Assassination of Royal Favourite
1628

A young army officer, Lieutenant Hammond, made a tour of southern England in the late summer of 1635. Travelling from Chichester, he paused on the top of Portsdown to enjoy the view and there 'breath'd, and tooke fresh ayre both from Sea and Land' before descending 'downe for Portsmouth, and so over a Bridge'. Some two miles from the town, however, on a highway near the sea, he wrote afterwards:

I espy'd a wofull Spectacle, which was the bones of that unfortunate Felton, hanging neere by in Chaines for his treacherous act, in giving the Duke a fatall stroke.

Buckingham House. From Gates

Unabashed, Lieutenant Hammond continued his journey and entered the town after due challenge and examination by the sentries on duty at the Town Gate. He then made his way down the High Street to the *Red Lion*, the well-known inn behind the parish church, where, he remarked, his hostess 'was briske, blith and merry, a hansome sprightly Lasse, fit for the company of brave Commaunders'. His route may have taken him past the *Greyhound* where the unfortunate duke in question – erstwhile royal favourite, George Villiers, duke of Buckingham – was indeed assassinated, on 23 August 1628, by former soldier John Felton.

The *Greyhound* was the home of Captain John Mason, a sometime speculator in the North American plantations, an adventurer and sea captain who had enjoyed particular success recently sailing under letters of marque in the Channel, picking up French prizes. It is more than likely that his prize money enabled him to purchase the *Greyhound,* possibly a former inn and now, one of the best houses in Portsmouth. There he established himself in due course as a man of substance and one of Portsmouth's leading citizens, a burgess and a member of the aldermanic bench. The house – No. 11 - still stands at the top of the High Street. It is much altered but it is nonetheless the place where Buckingham was murdered.

Mason had entered Buckingham's service first in 1625, as commissary general for the overseas force assembling in Plymouth for the expedition to Cadiz. He had his cousin Robert to thank for this position. Robert was Buckingham's secretary. Buckingham did not in fact accompany the fleet to Cadiz but Mason did, commanding the ship *Helen* of 200 tons. The expedition was a disaster but Mason emerged with some credit and a reputation as 'an honest, sufficient, careful officer'. He was therefore promoted on his return to play a key role in Buckingham's new military project, this time against the French.

Buckingham had been the favourite of the king's father, James I. He became a friend of the Prince of Wales during their incognito trip to Spain in 1623 to court the Infanta of Spain, an expedition commemorated in Portsmouth to this day by the replica bust of Charles set high on

The Duke of Buckingham. From Gates

the wall of the Square Tower at the bottom of the High Street. (The original bust is in the City Museum's collections).

As a young man, Buckingham captivated the old king. He was vital, good-looking, and a gallant courtier. James showered lands and honours on the young man. If Buckingham had confined his activities to the social life of the court, he would probably have survived to· a relatively distinguished old age, living on the profits of his glittering early years at court. Unfortunately, both for the country and for Buckingham himself, eventually, he showed what Dorothy Dymond has described in her study of John Mason and Buckingham in the *Portsmouth Paper* series as 'a fearless readiness, not only to govern England but to lead her into…dangerous adventure'.

It was all the more reckless as he was no statesman. He was concerned solely with personal glory, with feathering his own nest and furthering the interests of his own relations and friends. He had received no formal training at all, either for government or for soldiering but through the patronage first of an old, foolish and infatuated monarch, James I, and later, of James's stubborn oldest son and heir, Charles I, Buckingham assumed an impregnable position at court. 'All royal patronage', writes Dr Dymond, 'passed through his hands, all policy was decided by him, while he was responsible to no one but the master who wholeheartedly approved him'. There was criticism from some quarters, most notably from the House of Commons, but Buckingham was protected by his royal patrons who would not hear a word said against him.

The new expedition, this time against the French, was planned by Buckingham to expunge from people's memories all recollections of the Cadiz disaster. He resolved that he would himself lead an army and a navy to relieve the besieged Protestants – the Huguenots – of La Rochelle, regardless of the facts that he had no money for the enterprise, that the citizens of La Rochelle did not welcome particularly this prospect of assistance, and that the French themselves now had a useful navy of their own based nearby on the river Charente at Rochefort which was likely to provide effective opposition to any British naval force.

Mason was offered the important post of paymaster of the expeditionary army which assembled at Portsmouth in the early months of 1627. As paymaster, he was responsible for adminis-tering the finances of the expedition, providing the soldiers with their pay and equipment, and settling their billeting costs in the neighbourhood. It was a fraught and thankless task. Enormous sums were allocated to the enterprise by the privy council, but the money came through only irregularly and seldom in sufficient quantity to settle the debts of those officers carrying their men's wages and the sums due the billet hosts, who between them were effectively carrying the costs of the army. Mutiny became a distinct possibility.

George Goring, later Governor of Portsmouth, and at this time a young officer himself, wrote that the soldiers 'are all absolutely broke, both officers and men, and for this last week have been as near a mutiny as possible for want of money', and Mason reported that some billet hosts were as much as eight weeks in arrears of payment and therefore threatening to throw out their guests onto the streets. However, despite these problems, by 11 June 1627 a fleet of some one hundred ships had been assembled with over 7,800 soldiers including, ominously, for the future, a young lieutenant called John Felton. Buckingham sailed with his forces on this occasion and his presence caused a sensation wherever he was seen such was his reputation still as favourite, the king's intimate companion and the most powerful man in the kingdom after the king.

The plan was to seize the Isle de Ré, almost opposite La Rochelle, and use the island as a base for the attack. A landing was indeed effected, and Buckingham and his troops made their way across the island with little or no opposition to the town of St Martin and its strongly defended citadel. Buckingham was not a professional soldier though and he is described in the private journal of a subordinate officer at the time as arrogant and overbearing, looking only for personal glory and ignoring the advice of experienced soldiers. St Martin was besieged by land and sea but both sides soon ran short of supplies. The French did manage to get much-needed provisions through to their troops one dark and stormy night but fresh supplies for the besiegers were held up in Portsmouth by contrary winds.

Against the advice of his experienced officers Buckingham resolved to hold on and wait for those supplies. A final attempt to storm the citadel failed and, when news reached Buckingham that the French had mustered a force of some two thousand men and were marching across the island to meet him, he decided at last to leave. His troops were routed as he sought to embark them from the small island of Loix which was connected by a bridge to the Isle de Ré. Only half of his force of almost eight thousand men limped home to Plymouth and Portsmouth. It was another ignominious end to a foreign adventure.

Extraordinarily however, no sooner had he returned than Buckingham was making fresh plans to return to the scene of this, his most recent and most humiliating disaster. Between them, Buckingham and the king were blind to public sentiment, and the clamour about 'the great disaster' which Mason recorded 'had so dejected the hearts of men'. The returning troops were ordered to go back to their former lodgings while preparations began again to put a new fleet to sea. Mason himself set about salvaging what he could of the equipment brought ashore in Portsmouth by the soldiers. Muskets, pikes, swords and body armour were even stacked within the confines of his own home, the *Greyhound*. He had to deal as well with the sick and wounded. The most serious cases were taken by wagon to London to St Thomas's and St Bartholomew's hospitals. The less seriously wounded were boarded in Portsmouth.

As was to be expected, billet dues and the soldier's wages began to mount once more and there was no money left to meet these expenses. The tempers of the men and their hosts began to fray. The situation was no better in Plymouth where Mason found disaffected troops without officers running amok in the streets. It was an impossible situation which could only be solved with adequate supplies of money. He distributed what funds he had at his disposal on account which was just about enough to stop local people from throwing out their unwelcome guests. He returned wearily to Portsmouth, where the lack of any decent dry dock facilities was seriously hampering efforts to get ships ready to put to sea once again.

Matters came to a head in mid-December when a number of ship's companies resolved to march to London and demand their long overdue wages in person. The fear of insurrection in Portsmouth was such that martial law was declared. To compound the town's miseries, sick sailors brought ashore and billeted in the town brought pestilence into those households. Further consignments of men were therefore turned away, and when the mayor himself, Henry Holt, made two old properties of his own available, the seamen returned the 'kindness', as he reported ruefully afterwards, by taking the places apart.

A small expedition to La Rochelle put to sea in May 1628 led by Buckingham's brother-in-law, the Earl of Denbigh, but the expedition found the sea entrance blockaded and returned home. Buckingham resolved to lead a bigger expedition himself later in the year. Mason was still charged with conveying, billeting and embarking the army but as before money never followed promises and the previous complaints about the billeting system now swelled to a national outcry as municipal and county authorities across the country complained of the disorderly conduct of troops quartered in their communities. Matters came to a head in the House of Commons in early June, when the king was forced finally to agree to the Petition of Right. Parliament petitioned the king not to levy taxation without its consent, not to imprison people without cause shown, not to billet soldiers on civilians without their consent, and not to subject civilians to martial law.

A new invasion force was assembled finally by August 1628 with a fleet of almost sixty assorted ships. Portsmouth was overwhelmed now with soldiers, seamen and of course visitors. Those who were not yet on board were staying in local inns and lodgings or, if they were particularly important, in the homes of Portsmouth's leading citizens. To Captain John Mason fell the signal honour of entertaining the duke himself. Dr Dymond quotes some of the correspondence which passed between them. Mason was clearly extremely flattered:

> *Your Grace's lodging is prepared in my house here which will not only grace it and myself, but shall bind me perpetually to remain your Excellency's most humble devoted servant.*

It must indeed have been the proudest moment of his, Mason's, life. However, there were serious risks attendant in entertaining this man who, while he may have been the greatest man in England and the king's especial favourite, was also now the most unpopular – and threatened - man in the realm.

Rumours of invasion abounded, naval indiscipline was rife and most men's wages were still substantially in arrears. Many seamen and troops were also absconding in droves. Such was the explosive atmosphere that it was considered unwise for the king to take up residence in Portsmouth. The court established itself instead at Southwick House on the other side of Portsdown Hill. The anxieties of the king's advisers were not misplaced. An angry crowd of some three hundred seamen mobbed Buckingham's coach outside his lodgings on 16 August demanding pay. He was on his way to Southwick to attend the king. One man who attempted to pull Buckingham from the coach was actually apprehended by the duke himself.

After he had bundled the man into the house, Buckingham

spoke with the crowd, and believing that he had appeased them, he set off for Southwick but no sooner had he departed than the crowd stormed back up the High Street threatening now to tear down Mason's house if the prisoner was not released. To quiet the situation, Mason released the man. It was not the end of the incident though. When Buckingham returned from Southwick he saw his assailant on the street and had him re-arrested. Violence flared up again and, as he was led away, sailors attacked his guard. A team of officers turned out to put down this latest insurrection, assisted now by Buckingham himself on horseback with his own staff. Between them, they drove the seamen at sword point down to the sea and their ships, but not without considerable loss of life. It was estimated by onlookers that many were left dead or wounded. It was not a good start to the expedition.

More ominously, nemesis was approaching in the person of John Felton. According to Lake Allen in his *History of Portsmouth* published in 1817, Felton was 'a man of good family' but 'of a gloomy enthusiastic disposition'. He had served as a lieutenant under the duke in the ill-fated Isle de Ré expedition where he had witnessed the slaughter of English troops both during the last attempted assault on St Martin's citadel and later, in the ignominious retreat. His captain was killed in the retreat and Felton applied to Buckingham for the company but he was refused. He was also due some £80 back pay which was long overdue. Angered, he threw up his commission and retired from the army nursing a considerable personal grievance against Buckingham.

He returned to London where his family lived. He took lodgings and there, in June, he came across a copy of the recent House of Commons remonstrance, which was severely critical of Buckingham and the conduct of the war, in a scrivener's shop in Holborn. It expressed much of what he felt about Buckingham and 'it came into his mind that by killing the duke he should do his country great service'. Lake Allen reported that

he was now convinced it would be a meritorious action in the sight of heaven to murder him, whom the Parliament had accused as the author of all the misfortunes of his country.

Therefore, without further ado, Felton made his arrangements. He bid farewell to his family and set off for Portsmouth, having bought a knife on Tower Hill for ten pence, which he secreted in the lining of his pocket. Reportedly, he left word at a church to pray for a man 'grievously discontented in mind'. Walking, or securing rides where he could, he made his way down to Portsmouth. He spent the night of 22 August outside the town in a small village some three miles away, possibly in Kingston. The following morning he made his way into Portsmouth.

The duke was preparing to leave his lodgings to take news to the king at Southwick of rumours which had reached the town that La Rochelle had been relieved, although the contingent of French Protestant officers with him in Portsmouth, led by the Duke of Soubise, disputed this possibility strongly, and had exchanged angry words with Buckingham on the subject. Felton mingled unremarked and unchallenged in this crowd of French and English officers in the hallway of Mason's house, 'unknown among many and yet well known amongst many, as having been a lieutenant in the army'. And when Sir Thomas Fryer, a colonel in the army, exchanged a low bow with the duke, he was able to reach easily over Sir Thomas's shoulder and plunge his dagger into Buckingham's chest. According to Lake Allen

> *The knife with which the wound was inflicted, reached his heart, and without uttering any other words than 'the villain has killed me', he drew out the knife and immediately expired in a deluge of his own blood.*

It was not clear in the initial confusion exactly what had happened. No one saw who had delivered the blow and Felton had slipped away. Some thought Sir Thomas was responsible. Others believed that it was the French party, whose voices had been raised in fierce dispute with Buckingham shortly beforehand. In the midst of the confusion however, again according to Lake Allen

> a *hat was found near the door, in the inside of which was sewed a paper containing three or four lines of the remonstrance of the Commons, which declared Buckingham an enemy to the kingdom. All were now convinced that this hat belonged to the assassin, but there was a sufficient reason to think that he had escaped far enough during the tumult, not to be found without a hat. They were, however, mistaken; Felton never attempted to escape from justice, and he was soon perceived walking leisurely before the door, without his hat. He was immediately seized, confessed the murder, and seemed to triumph in the action.*

Interior of St Thomas's Church showing the Buckingham Memorial at the top of the chancel, mid nineteenth century.
Author's collection

Close-up of the Buckingham Memorial, c. 1906-7. PMRS

The soldiers who apprehended him were all for killing him on the spot. Apparently, he exposed his breast and invited them to proceed but the men's officers ordered them to put up their swords. Later, under questioning, he said that he struck the blow with the force of forty men, that he acted entirely on his own and further, he told his interrogators

> *that the resolution proceeded wholly from the impulse of his own conscience; and that if his hat was found, his motives would sufficiently appear; for, persuaded he should perish in the attempt, he had taken care to explain them, in order that no innocent person might suffer on his account.*

He was clearly still elated. However, reflection and confinement, wrote Lake Allen,

> *had great effect on the enthusiastic spirit of Felton; he seemed*

to recover from his delusion, expressed remorse for what he had done, and suffered death with composure and resignation.

He was questioned initially in Portsmouth but he was then taken to London for further questioning under torture. He was tried and convicted in due course in the King's Bench and sentenced to be hanged at Tyburn. The execution was carried out on 29 November 1628 and his body was brought back to Portsmouth where it was hung in chains on Southsea Common.

When he compiled his history in 1817, Lake Allen wrote that  'not many years since his gibbet was still visible; there are now however no remains left of it'. There is however a splendid monument to the Duke of Buckingham still standing in Portsmouth's Anglican cathedral. Buckingham is in fact buried in Westminster Abbey but his grieving sister, the Countess of Denbigh, had this monument with its soaring triumphant phoenix erected to the memory of one who 'possessed in an eminent degree the gifts of nature and fortune'!

Buckingham House, c. 1900. From Gates

The eastern end of the fortifications, as sketched in 1729 showing the obelisk on the beach where Felton's gibbet stood. From Gates

CHAPTER 10

'Jack the Painter'
1777

Many older members of Portsmouth's keen community of local historians will tell you that when they were small children before the Second World War, they actually saw the tobacco pipe stopper in Portsmouth's High Street museum, which was supposedly the mummified finger cut from the corpse of 'Jack the Painter', the man who tried to burn down Portsmouth dockyard in 1776. For many of them the memory of this grisly remain still exercised the same horrible fascination as it did almost seventy years before when they gingerly examined it. It was 'a hard-looking, yellowish object, fitted with a metal base and ring (for attaching to a watch-chain)', recalled former police inspector James Cramer.

'Jack the Painter' was in fact baptised James Aitken, He was not even known as 'Jack the Painter' during his life-time. He was known then as 'John the Painter' and he was known as such throughout the hue and cry which preceded his final arrest. He became 'Jack' only in death when his notoriety was advertised to an avid public, not only in his own confession, *The Life and Times of James Aitken,* dictated in Winchester gaol, and rushed through the press by an enterprising local printer, but in a stream of other lurid accounts of his life.

He was born in Edinburgh in 1752, one of twelve children of George and Magdalen Aitken. George Aitken was well-respected. He was a blacksmith and a burgess and was able to secure a good education for at least four of his boys, including James, at Heriot's Hospital. James left Heriot's after six years at the school and was apprenticed to a house-painter. He completed his seven-year apprenticeship successfully but it is clear from his surviving memoir that this is not what he had planned for a career. He had wanted to be a soldier but it had not proved possible to raise the sums necessary to secure him a commission. He also claimed to hold republican sympathies. He therefore embarked for London, 'in a fit of resentment', determined, in time-honoured fashion, to seek there fame and fortune.

As many young men, before and since, have discovered, the streets of London are not paved with gold. Aitken secured work as a painter but he soon became bored with this sort of life and fell into bad company. He lost what little money he had in 'vice and debauchery' and to fund these extravagances, he fell into a life of crime. He became a highwayman and a thief. He also crossed to North America to try his luck in the American colonies, where the settlers were becoming increasingly frustrated by the failure of successive British governments to acknowledge the particular difficulties of trying to administer what was in fact an emerging nation on the other side of the Atlantic.

Aitken claimed afterwards to have been present at the Boston Tea Party, when aggrieved colonists tipped quantities of tea into the harbour, but known facts about his perambulations in North America do not square with this romantic claim. Clearly he did not find, or was not prepared to work at finding, the sort of new life he wanted in the colonies, and he turned up again in England at the beginning of 1775, where he resumed his earlier career as a thief and robber.

He may also have enlisted under a false name at about this time, for he claimed afterwards that he stayed just long enough to secure his enlistment bonus before deserting. More importantly however it was during this time that he claimed that his early republican sympathies turned into impassioned support for the principles of what was now the American Revolution, and he determined that he would strike a blow for the American cause himself by destroying the six royal dockyards: Deptford and Woolwich on the Thames, Chatham and Sheerness on the Medway, Portsmouth and Plymouth. He calculated, very cleverly, that by knocking out Britain's capacity to repair and renew its fleets – the very effective means by which the country defended its shores and protected its vital trading enterprises – he would advance the American cause immeasurably.

'I spent two days in the contemplation of this malicious design', he wrote,

and promised myself immortal honour in the accomplishment of it. I beheld it in the light of a truly heroic enterprise, such as would never have been equalled to the end of time. I was

*persuaded it would entitle me to the first rank in America, and
flattered myself with the ambition of becoming the admiration
of the world.*

He was not alone in harbouring sympathies for the American
revolutionary cause. There was a most unlikely clandestine
figure in Portsmouth itself in the person of the Reverend
Thomas Wren, the minister of the Presbyterian church in the
High Street. He supported the ideals of the American
Revolution, and when a prison was established for captured
American seamen at Forton, on the Gosport side of Portsmouth
harbour, in 1777, he visited the imprisoned men regularly,
taking with him donations from other local sympathisers
including the ruling political oligarchs in Portsmouth, the
Carter family. It is also clear, from the surviving diaries of the
prisoners themselves, that he facilitated a number of escapes,
despite the great risks involved both for himself and for those he
helped. He gave the runaways sanctuary in his High Street
chapel in Portsmouth and then put them on the road to safe
houses in London. Once there it was not difficult for them to
find a passage on a boat prepared to cross clandestinely to the
French coast.

After the peace, in appreciation of his kindness and
generosity, the American Congress passed a vote of thanks to
Mr Wren. He resumed his normal ministry and died peacefully
in his home in Portsmouth in 1787. There would be no vote of
thanks from a grateful nation for James Aitken however nor
would he die peacefully in his bed mourned by his neighbours
and friends. To begin with, Aitken's treachery was discovered
during hostilities. His proposed scheme was also in a different
league altogether. He has been described recently as the first
British terrorist, an individual who committed acts of terror in
this country on behalf of a foreign power. He certainly prepared
his plans very carefully. He visited each dockyard site and drew
careful plans of their configuration, and where the storehouses
stood which would be his particular targets. He also noted very
carefully the state of security in each dockyard. Most
importantly, he designed an incendiary device specifically for
his purposes.

It is described in *The Life of James Aitken*. It was made of a
bottomless tin case:

which is made in a long square form. A little wooden box is made to fit the case, which having a hole through the centre, admits the bottom of a candle into it, which when lighted has vent and air by means of some small holes towards the top of the tin case or canister. The box is filled with combustibles of different kinds, which when the candle is nearly burnt out, take fire, and by means of the matches placed round, communicate the flames to everything they touch.

Aitken then went to Paris where he set out his scheme and described the preparations he had made to the American commissioner there, Silas Deane. Deane was careful not to endorse these proposals wholeheartedly. If they failed and he was implicated himself in the aftermath, it would do neither the American cause nor his own career any good at all. However if the scheme proceeded without being discovered then he, Deane, could not but benefit. He therefore gave Aitken a small sum of money and some limited support, including instructions on how to get in touch with a contact who might be useful in England.

Aitken now returned to England. He landed at Dover and made his way to Canterbury. There an unsuspecting tinsmith made several of his fire-starting devices and he proceeded to Portsmouth. He rented a room in the town on 6 December and now set about implementing his designs. He was able to negotiate his way easily into the dockyard. He was, after all, familiar with the lay-out of the various store-houses, having spent time reconnoitring there earlier in the year. He placed the first of his fire-starters in a hemphouse. He then made his way into a nearby ropehouse. He laid a slow-burning match here which he had also designed himself. It was made of paper and coated with charcoal and gunpowder. It led to hemp stuffed into the top of a bottle filled with turpentine. At this point – it was the end of the working day – he found himself locked in the ropehouse. He was freed by dockyard workers who heard him pounding on a door and accepted his excuse that he had wandered in there out of curiosity.

He returned to his lodgings in Portsmouth for the night and set off the following morning for the dockyard suburb of Portsea, where he found a new room. His plan was to return there for his possessions and set a diversionary fire after he had finished what he had set himself to do in the dockyard. He rented still another room with the intention of starting a fire there too. The next afternoon, 7 December, he tried to start the fire in the hemphouse but his matches were too damp and would not ignite. However, he was more successful in the ropehouse where his treated paper device ignited most satisfactorily. Panicked, he did not attempt to retrieve any of his possessions, nor start the fires he had set in his rented rooms. Instead he hitched a lift on a wagon which was leaving town. Abandoning his transport near Portsbridge, he was able to look back across fields to the distant town and dockyard and see flames lighting the early night sky.

The ropehouse was gutted but being built of brick was reconstructed within months, and little damage was done to adjoining buildings. Neither was any damage done to the five ships in dry dock for repairs, nor the three warships in various stages of construction on the building slips. But it had been a close call. The king, the government, the Navy Board and the general public were appalled, and impatient for any news which might identify the cause of the fire and any culprit or culprits. James Gambier, a member of the Navy Board and the resident commissioner in Portsmouth dockyard began inquiries immediately.

It was not long before a possible lead emerged. Gambier was told that a man known as 'John the Painter' who had been working in the Titchfield area earlier in the year had been seen in the dockyard on the day of the fire and had in fact been found locked in the now gutted ropehouse the previous evening. Inquiries in Titchfield elicited a passable description of the suspect which was circulated widely in the new year in newspaper advertisements throughout southern England. Official anxiety had increased considerably when a series of fires on Bristol's waterfront, on the night of 15-16 January 1777 and some three nights later, did more damage than had been done in Portsmouth before Christmas. Evidence also seemed to point to the fires being the work of the same hand. In addition Aitken's fire-starting device had been discovered now in the Portsmouth hemphouse.

Aitken had in fact made his way successfully to London after he had fired the ropehouse in Portsmouth. There he had met finally with Samuel Deane's contact, who turned out to be a medical practitioner, one Dr Edward Bancroft. Neither Aitken nor Deane was ever aware though that Bancroft was a double agent. He therefore did nothing to help Aitken but on the other hand he did not report Aitken's activities to the authorities despite the widespread publicity. Frustrated and angered by this lack of support Aitken had set off for Plymouth to continue his

fire-starting enterprise. It did not prove so easy to start fires
there however so he had turned northwards and decided to try
his hand in Bristol with its formidable commercial shipping
trade. The country was now badly frightened. Where would
'John the Painter' strike next?

The advertisement in the *Hampshire Chronicle* was typical of
the advertisements placed in local newspapers:

> *Whereas there is strong reason to suspect that the Ropehouse in
> his Majesty's Dock-yard at Portsmouth was, on the 7th
> December last, most wickedly and maliciously set on fire, and
> whereas several attempts (some of which have taken effect) have
> been made to set fire to the city of Bristol, and as there is reason
> to suppose the incendiary or incendiaries may have been the
> same in both cases, the following description of a person who
> was seen in the Rope-house in Portsmouth yard on the day the
> said fire happened, and whose conduct was suspicious, is now
> published, in hopes that, on his apprehension, some light may
> be thrown on these two dreadful transactions.*

A description followed. The suspect was called John and he was
a painter. He had reportedly worked the previous summer in
Titchfield. He was about twenty-five or twenty-six years old,
and about five feet seven inches high, rather thin in person and
face, smooth-faced and with a fair complexion. He wore his own
hair which was of a light and sandy colour. The clothes he was
wearing on 7 December 1776 were described in detail. He had
on that day 'a chocolate coloured surtout coat faded, a rusty hat,
rather smartly cocked, with a fantail behind'. A reward of £50
was offered for his apprehension. The Admiralty subsequently
increased this to £1,000.

Aitken was in fact apprehended before the end of January.
Together, two individuals converged on the prey. James Lowe, a
linen draper of Calne, Wiltshire was robbed by Aitken. His wife
recalled a man – a possible suspect - loitering outside their shop
the day before the robbery and was able to describe him to her
husband, who set off after him. At the same time, John Dalby
who kept the Andover bridewell, had read the advertisements
placed by the authorities in the newspapers and asked around
amongst his neighbours whether they had seen anyone
answering to the description. Someone thought they had and
Dalby set off in hot pursuit of the possible suspect in the
direction he was believed to be travelling. Dalby caught up with

him first at Hook, near Odiham. Lowe arrived shortly afterwards. Together they escorted Aitken back to Odiham where he was detained by a local justice of the peace on suspicion of burglary.

Only then did Lowe realise that the man who had robbed him was in fact 'John the Painter'. He notified the Navy Board of the news in a brief note as follows:

> *On Monday the 27 instant, I lodged in Odiham Jail near Basingstoke Hampshire a Man for Housebreaking which answers to an Advertisement in the news Papers relative to a man setting Fire to the Ropehouse in his Majesty's Dock Yard at Portsmouth, the man answers the description in every respect. I found on him a loaded Pistol with Shot, a Tinderbox Pistol, a Vial Bottle of spirits of Turpentine, a bundle of Matches dipped in Brimstone and a box of exceeding fine Tinder made of Silk.*

Witnesses were rounded up hurriedly by the Navy Board and Gambier in the Portsmouth area including Aitken's former landlady, one Elizabeth Boxall. Several were taken to Odiham and confirmed that the man lodged there in the town gaol was indeed 'John the Painter'. He was therefore transferred to London to be examined by Bow Street magistrates. Aitken refused to cooperate with his questioners. He denied all the charges levelled at him, claimed not to know any of the witnesses and would admit nothing. He was also still known only by his alias. Eventually he foolishly confided in a fellow housepainter, James Baldwin, who had been introduced to him quite deliberately by the chief magistrate, Sir John Fielding. Baldwin reported everything that the trusting Aitken, believing that he was conversing with a fellow-radical and American sympathiser, told him. Thus Aitken incriminated himself. He was charged with arson, not treason, as it would be easier to secure a conviction, and was transferred now to Winchester where he was indicted formally by the local grand jury and the date of the trial was set.

The trial took place on 6 March in the thirteenth-century Great Hall of Winchester Castle, which still stands at the top of Winchester's High Street. By 7.00 am on the day there was no space left for onlookers in the hall, such was the excitement generated by the event. Aitken denied all the charges in court but Baldwin's testimony sealed his fate. He was found guilty and condemned to death. He was ordered to be taken to Portsmouth where he would be hanged on 10 March 1777. He left the court still refusing to acknowledge his guilt but he had a change of heart shortly afterwards and, before he was taken down to Portsmouth, he dictated a confession.

On the morning of 10 March he was taken, shackled, by carriage to Portsmouth. He was hanged from the mizzen mast of the *Arethusa*, which had been erected for the occasion not far from the dockyard gate near the Common Hard in front of a crowd, it was claimed, of almost twenty thousand. His body was lowered eventually and, still shackled, placed in gibbet irons and hung on a gibbet at Blockhouse Point. His bare and bleached bones swung there in the cage at the harbour mouth for many years as an awful warning to anyone who might contemplate a similar undertaking.

His mummified finger was lost when the High Street museum was destroyed during the first blitz on the city on the night of 10-11 January 1941 but several of the items taken off him by John Dalby when he arrested him – his awl, powder flask and bottle of turpentine – came into the ownership of the Museum and Records Service in 1963.

'James Aitken. Alias Jack the Painter' as drawn for the London Magazine, *March 1777.* PMRS 1371/1974.

CHAPTER 11

The Execution of a Traitor
1782

On 24 August 1782 possibly one of the most gruesome events in the town's history took place near Southsea beach, a little to the east of today's Clarence Pier, and probably on or near the site of Felton's gibbet. There had been bathing machines here since the 1770s, and within a generation the distinctive and elegant Landport, Hampshire, King's and Bellevue Terraces would be rising nearby, conveniently situated for the new pump room, baths and reading room, overlooking the sea where the pier is now situated.

'Gosport, The Entrance to Portsmouth Harbour', c. 1829 by J M W Turner. PMRS

The drama which took place on the beach that August afternoon had nothing to do however with Southsea's future as a watering place. It had everything to do rather with the town's role as a royal dockyard and garrison town; a town which had been responsible for supplying this country with the 'sinews of war' since the late twelfth century. With James Aitken's bones in sight, swinging in chains from the gibbet at Blockhouse Point, at the harbour mouth, another man was drawn on a sledge early in the morning from the town gaol to another gibbet and there, before a crowd reckoned, improbably, to number 100,000, he was hanged, disembowelled and quartered.

The scenes which took place afterwards beggar belief. Onlookers scrabbled to get hold of a piece of the body. Fingers to make pipe-stoppers were fought over keenly and handkerchiefs were thrust into the blood. A Gosport man – Buck Adams, the keeper of the Gosport bridewell - reportedly made off with the victim's head which he kept in spirits in a specially-commissioned glass vessel on the counter of his beerhouse for many years. The military escort, always present at public executions, ostensibly to prevent such scenes developing, tried somewhat ineffectually to restore order and was pelted with stones for its efforts. The proceedings deteriorated then into a vicious free-for-all in which a number of people were badly injured.

Who was this man whose barbaric end prompted such mayhem? He was another Scot, a man called David Tyrie, who was found guilty of treason at a trial which took place on 10 August 1782. The trial took place, as Aitken's had only a few years before, in the Great Hall of the Castle at Winchester. Not a great deal is known about Tyrie. He seems to have come to London originally as a servant and worked there as a clerk for a stationer called Vowle. He then moved into some sort of trading business of his own which was not particularly successful and eventually he took up a post in the Navy Office at Portsmouth. Interestingly, like Aitken before him, there was an American connection. Some newspaper accounts said that he was in fact an American. His father, who was Scottish, had fled to America in 1745 to escape possible retribution for the part he had played in the rising of that year. Did that episode and its aftermath shape indelibly the younger Tyrie's life and times?

Tyrie was charged on two separate counts of treason: firstly, that he had sent the French details of British ships and their movements and secondly, that he had colluded 'unlawfully and

David Tyrie.
From Gates

traitorously' with the king's enemies. He pleaded not guilty to both charges but, despite the best efforts of his counsel, the evidence against him was cumulatively overwhelming.

The first witness, a woman called Mrs Hervey who kept a school in New Scotland Yard, testified that on 13 February 1782 a female who proved subsequently to be Tyrie's wife asked her to look after a packet of papers. Mrs Hervey was very suspicious and opened the packet. She was concerned by what she saw and took the packet to Mr Jonathan Page who examined the documents in the packet closely. In his view they related to treasonable matters and he arranged for the packet to be sent to the Secretary of War who advised that they be sent to the Admiralty.

The next two witnesses, Mr John Vowle and Mr John Palmer, were shown the packet of documents. They confirmed that the writing on the documents was that of David Tyrie. Vowle was in fact Tyrie's former employer, the London stationer. These two gentlemen were followed by Mr Thomas Flint who was employed with Tyrie in the Navy Office in Portsmouth. His evidence was crucial. He was handed the documents seen by the two previous witnesses and said that they were similar to material in his office. He then produced a book – 'An Account of the readiness for the Sea of His Majesty's Ships and Vessels under Repair, and of those Building and Rebuilding, and of such as lie in Harbour' - which detailed work done to naval ships. He demonstrated that the documents in question seemed to be identical copies of some of the pages in his book.

The documents – mostly lists – allegedly in Tyrie's handwriting, were read out to the court: details of ships and their condition at merchant's yards – private builders – at Portsmouth, Plymouth, Woolwich, Sheerness and Harwich; a list of Navy ships in numerical order with details of their armament, and a list in another hand but endorsed by Tyrie 'Going to Mahon or Africa, to be met by the Convoy with Troops.' Other lists, most itemising details of different ships, were addressed to correspondents in Ostend, Boulogne and Paris.

There were further documents advising on where it was possible to obtain detail about naval ships. The writer advised that the information could be obtained from a variety of sources: the Navy Office, Admiralty, Navy Ordnance and Victualling Offices, and of course from the dockyards themselves. The dockyards, he suggested, were the best sources of information and that 'a communication with an intelligent person at each of the dockyards is the best channel for procuring and keeping an exact State of the Navy'. Another document actually suggested possible sums – five guineas a month - to be paid to such persons as well as other expenses likely to be incurred in setting up an intelligence network. It was alleged that this last document was in Tyrie's handwriting.

The next individual into the witness box was Mr William James, a merchant navy captain, whom Tyrie endeavoured to employ in February 1782, ostensibly to obtain wine from Boulogne for ships bound for the East Indies. They met on Gosport beach. At the time, James said that he advised Tyrie that the wind was in the wrong direction for a voyage to Boulogne, but that Tyrie said this would not matter. Cherbourg would do just as well. Interestingly James remarked that he was not unfamiliar with Cherbourg but that it was nevertheless hazardous to attempt to enter an enemy port in wartime. Tyrie apparently dismissed this as a problem and said that he would let James have details of signals he could fly which would enable him to enter the harbour at Cherbourg safely.

James also testified that on another occasion, he believed on 17 February, he visited Tyrie's lodgings and saw Tyrie, and a woman that he believed was Tyrie's wife, sat together at a table. They were both writing. Later Tyrie gave James a packet of letters which James identified as the packet then produced and shown him in court. James also told the court that at the same time as he gave James the packet of letters, Tyrie handed him a note of the signals he was to run up to secure entry to the port of Cherbourg. He also advised James that once the signals were seen from the shore, a boat would come out to him and take off the packet of papers. He would then be allowed ashore.

Clearly alarmed, James handed the packet of letters to a Captain Harrison the following morning. Mr William Harrison was called next into the witness box. He told the court that when he opened the packet of letters he saw that one was addressed to the Minister of Marine in Paris. He therefore went straight to London and delivered the packet to Mr Fraser, Lord Stormont's secretary. Lord Stormont was Secretary of State in the Northern Department. Mr William Fraser was then called as a witness. He told the court that he examined the contents of the packet of letters brought to him by Mr Harrison. The address on the front cover – to Captain James – was in the prisoner's handwriting. There were seven documents in the packet and they were read out in court. There were several seemingly innocuous letters relating to the purchase of different quantities of wine, spirits and tea from suppliers in Cherbourg and Ostend, and the arrangements to be made for paying for these orders. But there was another letter addressed to a senior naval officer in Cherbourg asking him to forward to Paris a letter for the Minister of Marine, which contained a detailed list of convoys assembling at Spithead with their destinations and wind directions.

Other witnesses called gave similarly damning evidence. Printed lists of naval ships were found about his person when he was first arrested. Quantities of suspicious material were found in his lodgings. There were papers on the canopy above his bed, others in a trunk and a number loose about his room. They included a list of ordnance stores at different forts, lists of the ships at Woolwich as well as other ports including Portsmouth, and a document setting out the state of the national debt.

Mr James Mailstone informed the court that Tyrie asked him to send him an account of all the warships which came into Portsmouth or sailed from Spithead, and details of the convoys. He understood from Tyrie that what he was doing was quite legitimate but became alarmed when Tyrie pressed him hard for this information. He therefore delayed sending it and sometimes even supplied false information. He gave the information to a Captain Bowles. He understood that Mr Bowles sailed to Boulogne or some other French port to collect wine for East India ships. He received at least £30 from Tyrie for supplying this information.

Tyrie's counsel made a robust speech in defence of his client. He pointed out that not all the documents were in his client's handwriting and that none of the documents had in fact been found on his person. Further, he said, there were a number of publications containing lists of naval ships available for sale in bookshops across the kingdom. Lists of ships had been found in a packet of documents containing treasonable material but in his view there was no evidence to link Tyrie with this packet. Yes, there was evidence that Tyrie may have been engaged in smuggling French wines and spirits but this was not evidence that he was engaged in treasonable activities. The treasonable letter in question was not even in his handwriting.

Despite counsel's best efforts the jury made up its mind very quickly. They brought in a verdict of 'Guilty' and the Judge pronounced sentence: that he, Tyrie, would be returned to the gaol from whence he had come (in fact this would be the Portsmouth gaol)

> *and from thence you are to be drawn, upon a hurdle, to the place of execution; and there you are to be hanged by the neck; and, being alive, to be cut down, and your privy members to be cut off, and your bowels to be taken out of your belly, and there burnt, you being alive; and your head to be cut off, and your body to be divided into four quarters; and that your head and quarters be disposed of where his Majesty shall think fit.*

It was also known that the French were assembling an invasion fleet, had plans to land troops on the Sussex coast and, in a flanking movement, attempt to seize Portsmouth from the north. The British government was well aware that the French were trying to collect what information they could on the disposition of ships and troops in Portsmouth from British seamen who fell into their hands, smugglers, the crews of merchant men captured by privateers operating almost unhindered now in the English Channel and sometimes, from renegade naval officers and seamen. It was also clear, not only in this case but from other incidents which were brought to the notice of the government, that there were French espionage rings operating in this country. Tyrie would never admit that he had any accomplices but there were suspicions that he did to the very end, and that some of them might be very highly placed in the machinery of government. In short, these were perilous times and the sentence meted out to David Tyrie reflected current anger and frustration with events both at home and abroad.

Tyrie meanwhile was returned to Newgate Prison in London, from where he had been taken to Winchester for his trial. There he attempted to end his own life with a razor which he had secreted on his person, but he was prevented from doing so by his warders who discovered what he was up to in time. There were rumours of an attempt at escape but it came to nothing and on 17 August he was transferred to Winchester gaol. There he was involved in an escape bid with other prisoners, which seems to have been hatched before his trial began but again, it came to nothing. Interestingly he had promised to take with him to France those people who would provide him with the means – the tools – to effect his escape. He also promised them pensions of £100 a year.

He was brought by coach from Winchester to Portsmouth early on the morning of 24 August. There he was handed over to the mayor and other borough officials. He was placed on the sledge and drawn to the place of execution. There he was hanged and after twenty-two minutes, the body was lowered. His head was cut off, his heart was taken out and burnt and his genitalia were cut off. (The judicial system still persisted in the belief that the heart, the organs of generation and the entrails were the seats of treasonable thought and should therefore be made clean by fire). Tyries's body was then quartered. The parts were not distributed across the country to be placed in prominent public places as an awful warning, as had been the custom in earlier times. They were placed in a coffin which, so one story goes, was buried amongst the stones on the nearby beach. Popular wisdom also has it that, after the official party had left, a group of sailors dug up the coffin and cut the remaining parts into souvenirs which were taken off in triumph to their ships. The reporter from the *Hampshire Chronicle* was deeply shocked and sickened by what he witnessed.

MISCELLANEA

CHAPTER 12

The 'Customs and Usages of Portsmouth'

Early History

Portsmouth was given criminal jurisdiction within its own boundaries in its first royal charter of 1194. However, the earliest detailed references to local law and order issues occur in a manuscript document in the City Museum and Records Office described as the 'Customs and Usages of Portsmouth'. It seems to be in the handwriting of Thomas Whitehorn who was Portsmouth Clerk to the Portsmouth and Sheet Turnpike Trust between 1727 and 1732. The British Museum advised local historian Robert East at the end of the nineteenth century that it was probably copied from a late fourteenth or early fifteenth century document. More recently a mid-sixteenth century date has been attributed to it but from internal evidence such as personal names, it is generally agreed that the document was drafted originally in the late thirteenth century if not even earlier.

Harry Le Pesuner who is mentioned in the text was certainly a bailiff in the 1270s, and a John son of Philip who is also mentioned was reeve between 1245 and 1270 according to the records of nearby Southwick Priory. The word reeve is Old English. Essentially it means one of high rank with a local jurisdiction. By the early fourteenth century the reeve had become the mayor and as such he presided over the borough courts and the administration of justice in the township with a modest team of officials including two constables.

The document deals initially with the transfer of power each year from one mayor and his officers to a new mayor, and the safe delivery to the new team of the common seal, the town records and the weights and measures. There then follows for the first time information on the treatment meted out to wrongdoers. By the mid thirteenth century criminal matters in the town of Portsmouth came up before the Court of View of Frankpledge which, with the Court Leet, was the oldest of the borough courts.

Derived from the ancient pre-Conquest arrangement of suretyship, the frankpledge system was a rudimentary police system by which persons were made mutually responsible for each other's behaviour. All over the age of twelve were required to be in collective suretyship in units of ten or twelve. Frequently whole villages or townships – as in Portsmouth - formed such a unit. If an individual in the group or town or village was suspected of a crime or misdemeanour, it was the duty of his neighbours to produce the miscreant in court. By the late thirteenth century these tasks had devolved in Portsmouth to the mayor and his small group of assistants, drawn from amongst the burgesses, who, between them, supervised the proceedings of the courts. They heard the presentments of the twelve members of the jury, summoned to answer the questions put to them concerning misdemeanours such as encroachments, affrays and bloodshed, breaches of the peace, and offences affecting trade in the town as defined in the Statute of Frankpledge of 1325:

> *Of Walls, Houses, Dikes, and Hedges set up or beaten down to*
>   *annoyance.*
> *Of Bounds withdrawn and taken away.*
> *Of Ways and paths opened and stopped.*
> *Of Waters turned or stopped, or brought from their right course.*
> *Of Breakers of Houses, and of their Receivers.*
> *Of Common Thieves and of their Receivers.*
> *Of Petty Larcons, as of Geese, Hens, or Sheafs.*
> *Of Thieves that steal Clothes, or of Thieves that do pilfer*
>   *Clothes through Windows and Walls.*
> *Of such as go in Message for Thieves.*
> *Of Cries levied and not pursued.*
> *Of Bloodshed, and of Frays made.*
> *Of Escapes of Thieves or Felons.*
> *Of Persons outlawed returned, not having the King's Warrant.*
> *Of Women ravished, not presented before the Coroners.*
> *Of Clippers and Forgers of Money.*
> *Of Treasure found...*

Sessions Court

Business at the Court Leet was relatively straightforward. There, as they would have been at the court baron of a lord of a manor, tenants were admitted to town lands and took oaths to be true tenants. During the seventeenth and eighteenth centuries the criminal work of these courts was assumed gradually by the Justices of the Peace who came to prominence in Elizabeth I's reign, sitting in meetings of the Sessions Court which, in a borough like Portsmouth, met twice a year. The justices met four times a year in the counties – at Quarter Sessions.

Few original early records survive. They were probably destroyed in one of the devastating French raids on the town in the later Medieval period. A number of documents were also 'abstracted' from the Muniment Room in the Town Hall between 1775 and 1820 according to Robert East. A rare example of a presentment relating to an affray exists in the earliest surviving Elections and Sessions Book. At a court held 22 June 1545 the twelve jurors presented

upon their oath that Roger Walton on the [illegible] *day in the xxxvi year (1544-5) of Henry VIII by force and arms beat*

The Town Hall and Market House erected in 1739 but demolished in 1836. A number of the town's records were stolen from this building in the late eighteenth century. PMRS *wounded and ill treated John Reynolds servant of William Young at Portsmouth in the house of the said William so that his life was despaired of, against the peace of the aforesaid Sovereign Lord the King, and for drawing the weapon is fined v s. and for breach of the peace vi s. viii d. and for the bloodshed vi d. according to the custom of the town, and therefore the Chamberlain is ordered to levy the said sums to the use of the Town.*

Fortunately the 'Customs and Usages of Portsmouth' document and its predecessors survived French raids and antiquarian thieves. It looks back to the ancient rough justice of the early Middle Ages, and even earlier times, when punishment was tailored to fit the crime. If convicted, thieves who took goods up

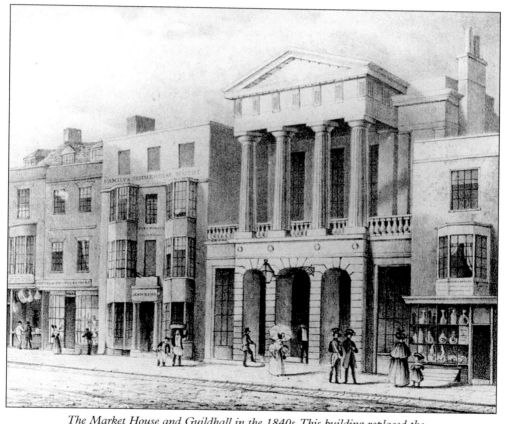

The Market House and Guildhall in the 1840s. This building replaced the eighteenth century Town hall. PMRS

to the value of 12*d*. would have their ear nailed to the pillory, and could choose then whether to have the ear cut off or to tear it off themselves. Dishonest trading such as breaking the Assize of Bread, an ordinance of 1266 which fixed the price of bread and ale, or any other craft offence, also put offenders in the pillory. Scolds were liable to be immersed in the Camber in the cucking or ducking stool:

Also if ther be any Chiders or Scoldys they be put in the Kokyng stole and late them fall yn to the Cambyr.

Thieves who stole goods presumably of greater value than 12*d* were branded and their eyes put out. If the thief was a woman, her 'teeys', or nipples, were cut off. If a man put to death another man, he would be burnt to death at *Cattecleffe*, an area believed at one time to be on the site of the oldest part of the present Portsmouth Naval Base but thought now to be in the Camber area. A woman who slew a man was tied to a stake at *Cattecleffe* at low water and left there for the rising tide to 'ov'flowe her'.

The nature of the crimes committed by local people over the centuries differs little from those described originally in the Statute of Frankpledge, as the following late seventeenth century list of Sessions cases heard before the mayor and two of his assistants, in their capacities as Justices of the Peace, demonstrates:

John Gawler *bound over about a false indenture.*

John Frith *bound to prosecute his Traverse itt is for abuseing the Mayor and all the Justices.*

Elizabeth Wallice *bound to prosecute her Traverse shee is indicted for being a Comon Scold.*

John Rickman *bound to prosecute his Traverses one Indictment was for useing the Trade of a Desteler the other for retaileing grocery wares.*

William Mellersh *bound over for receiving Iron stolen from their Maties carryages and to answear an Indictment found against him for permitting hoggs to runn about the streets contrary to the Constitucons &c.*

Mary Spinkes *bound over for abuseing Captain Brouncker one of the Justices, &c.*

Henry Belfielde, George Deacon gent, John Hanam, Jos: Grigge, James Wottle *bound to answer for Nusances &c.*

Frances Merreweather *bound over for abusing Mr. Mayor.*

John Besant *committed by Mr. Mayor for stealeing a flitch of Bacon of the value of : 10 d.*

John Burgen *bound to the peace for beateing and wounding his wife.*

Thomas Fullham *bound over for begetting Mary Harper with child shee is not delivered.*

Sarah Hopsonn *bound over for beateing and wounding of Martha Bone.*

John Grey *Committed by Mr Mayor for forgeing of a Certificate and fraudulently receiveing divers summes of money &c.*

Irregular trading, fornication, theft, bastardy, abusing authority, bribery, assault, keeping bawdy houses, gambling, sabbath breaking, disloyalty, riot, treason, drunkenness, unlawful religious assembly, wife beating, arson, blasphemy, receiving stolen goods, inciting mutiny, dangerous riding, slander, illegal hunting, sheltering vagrants, witchcraft and adultery were only some of the offences which Portsmouth people were charged with over the ensuing centuries. The official records are usually fairly bald accounts of what took place, but the advent of popular newpapers towards the end of the eighteenth century introduces for the first time a whole new dimension: crime reporting.

Vivid accounts appear now in the local newspapers of stories such as the one reported in the *Hampshire Telegraph* in February 1798 of the thirteen-year-old boy who had been stolen from his parents four years before and was being detained illegally by a chimney-sweeper in Epsom, Surrey, and the account of a smart piece of work by local magistrates in December 1799. The servant of a Russian officer was assaulted at the rear of the *Fountain* inn in the High Street and robbed of £100 by a gang led by the notorious 'Shepton Mallet Jack':

> *The alarm being given soon afterwards, a search was made during the night, and seven men and women were apprehended by the extraordinary activity and vigilance of the Constables, acting under a police as well-regulated as any in the kingdom, and what is further to their credit, although the offenders had taken different routes, to the distance of eight or nine miles, nearly the whole of the money was recovered and restored to its owner.*

A splendid fracas was reported in the *Hampshire Telegraph* in May 1843 when Mr Dennis Fagan of the Coastguard Service was patrolling in the Lumps Lane and Southsea Castle area. Seven men jumped over a bank and made him a prisoner. They tied his hands together and turned him on his face in the sand. More men now joined the party, about twenty-five, it was reported. A boat – a galley – approached and the gang ran down the beach to help heave it ashore, assuming it contained their brother-smugglers. When the boat was finally pulled in to the shore, to their horror, they found it contained a naval patrol. A pitched battle took place and a number of people were arrested.

In a similar vein, almost a hundred years later, the paper reported the story of the lone bank raider. On the morning of 29 March 1926 a bank employee of Lloyd's Bank, Copnor Bridge, was working quietly behind the counter when a man entered, drew a pistol and demanded cash. The cashier drew a bundle of notes from a drawer and passed them across the counter, the man seized them and ran out of the building. The cashier gave chase whereupon the robber turned and fired a shot at him. The bullet hit a wall fortunately. The thief ran out into Milton Road and along Hayling Avenue in the direction of the brickfields. There he snatched a bicycle from a workman and threatened more pursuers with his pistol.

The chase continued across Kingston Recreation Ground and into Byerley Road. At this point Police Sergeant Hopkinson arrived, just as the robber was knocked off his bicycle by a van. The man got up from the wreckage of his bicycle and fired at the men in the van. The enterprising Sergeant now commandeered a lorry and continued the chase along Penhale Road. As the lorry drew level with the fleeing man, the Sergeant threw himself from the vehicle and tackled the robber to the ground. Another policeman, Inspector Warren, now on the scene as well, helped overpower the man who was later charged with armed robbery of £50, shooting at the bank employee with intent to kill, and shooting at the two men in the van

One of the saddest cases of all however must be the story of the young woman who was buried in Wymering churchyard on 9 August 1772. There is no reference in the burial register to the manner of her death, but her stone lies on the west side of the church building and tells the story of a country girl who loved too well:

> *In Memory of Elizabeth*
> *Harrison, who Departed this*
> *Life August the 7th 1772,*
> *Aged 27 years.*
> *All you my Friends that this*
> *way passeth by*
> *Observe the adjacent field*
> *there shot was I,*
> *In bloom of Youth I had no*
> *thought of Death,*
> *So sudden I was forced to*
> *yield my breath.*
> *Therefore I'd have you to*
> *prepare your way*
> *For Heaven's high Summons*
> *all Men must obey.*

It seems that the young woman fell in love with a man who lived at Little Wymering Farm. He did not return her love but still she followed him from field to field as he went about his work. Finally one day he had had enough and he shot her as she trailed after him. He was tried at the Assizes, condemned and brought back to Wymering, where he was hanged from a tree near the scene of his crime.

The Assizes

Serious criminal offences – cases which might involve the death penalty – were not handled by local Sessions Courts. Such offences included homicide, infanticide, theft of goods over the value of one shilling (stolen goods were often valued at less than one shilling to avoid making the offence a capital one), highway robbery, rape, assault, coining, forgery and witchcraft. These cases were sent to the Assizes at Winchester. The Assize court met in the Great Hall and you can still see the trap door in the floor which leads down stairs to the cells below. They are not open to the public but there are photographs on display nearby of the cells and adjoining passages, through which the prisoners were led up to the courtroom above. The word 'assize' comes from the Old French for 'sittings', in this case for the 'sitting' of a court.

At the Assizes travelling royal justices met twice a year on regional circuits to hear serious criminal and civil cases. The process began in the thirteenth century. A pair of judges would cover a circuit which was made up of a group of counties. Hampshire was part of the Western Circuit which stretched from Surrey as far as Devon and Cornwall. Originally these courts dealt with property disputes but they came in due course to deal with criminal cases as well.

Punishment

Corporal punishment – flogging – and a fine was the usual punishment handed down for offences dealt with in the local Sessions Court. Robert East calculated that between 1698 and 1781 one hundred and twenty men and ninety-eight women were whipped as part of their sentence. Five or six were men or women who had been sentenced for vagrancy being found begging within the town. The rest were convicted for a range of offences, the most usual being the theft of goods worth less than a shilling. There was no difference in the punishment handed down whether the offender was male or female. Sometimes a certain number of stripes – anything between fifteen and forty – were stipulated to be given by the constable or beadle with 'a Catt of nine Tayls' but in the majority of cases offenders were flogged on their bared backs until their bodies were bloody. Punishment was administered either in the local prison or in public *e.g.* at the whipping posts in the market place in the High Street or near the cage on the Common(where offenders were apprehended in what was later Ordnance Row, Portsea, and where remnants of the stocks still stood in the 1860s). Sometimes the prisoner was flogged from one part of the town to another: from the gaol to the end of Point and back; from the dockyard gate, now Victory Gate, to Pudshole, now St James's Street, or from the gaol to the Landport Gate.

Occasionally the magistrates tailored the punishment to fit the particular crime. A man who stole three iron bolts from the dockyard weighing altogether about ten pounds was ordered to receive forty lashes at the dockyard gate with the three iron bolts tied round his neck, and a woman who had been convicted of stealing from two separate individuals was ordered to receive twenty lashes on each count: the first on the Saturday after her trial, and the second on the following Tuesday 'till her body be bloody'. The constable or beadle was paid a fee of sixpence for each man or woman thus flogged.

After the flogging the prisoner was usually brought back to the gaol and incarcerated there until the 'ffee' *i.e.* the fine was paid. Few of the warrants authorizing the whipping of an offender survive but Robert East published a good example in his *Extracts from Records in the possession of the Municipal Corporation of the Borough of Portsmouth* in 1891:

> *To the Constables of the said Burrough and the Liberties thereof, and every of them And also to the Comon Beadle of the said Burrough.*

> *Whereas at his Majesties Sessions of the Peace held at the Guildhall in and for the said Burrough on the day of the date hereof Elizabeth Smith, singlewoman, stands indicted and convicted for the felonious taking and stealing within the said Burrough one Holland apron of the value of nine pence the goods and chattles of Elizabeth Knight, widow, and thereupon the said Court gave Judgement that the said Elizabeth Smith should return to the Gaol from whence she came and there remain untill Saturday next between the hours of Eleven and Twelve of the Clock in the fforenoon at which time she is to be brought to the publick whipping post in the Market Place of the said Burrough and to be stript from the middle upwards and then fixt to the said whipping post and there receive Twenty Lashes with a Cat of Nine Tails from the hands of the Comon Beadle on her naked Back and till the same shall be Bloody and then return to the said Gaol and there remain until her ffees are paid. These are therefore in his Majesties name to will and require you and each and every of you to cause the said Judgement to be put in Execution of which you are not to fail at your perils. Dated in the said Sessions the Fourteenth day of October in the year of our Lord 1736.*

> *Examined by George Huish Clerk of the peace of the said Burrough.*

The Borough Gaol

The gaol was in the High Street. It was known as the White House. It had stood there from at least the mid-sixteenth century when the Borough Chamberlain was charged to organise repairs to the building. Prison at this time and until well into the nineteenth century, was a place where you were held before your trial or while awaiting punishment. It was rarely a punishment in its own right and Portsmouth's gaol was certainly not designed to hold large numbers of people. The White House occupied a domestic building plot on the east side of the High Street, near the Pembroke Road junction on the site occupied subsequently by the *Crown* inn and later by Lloyds Bank. The nineteenth century local medical practitioner and keen local historian, Henry Slight, described the building as follows:

It was a pointed fronted house, with small square iron grated casements; in front was a row of iron palisades, the door being in the centre through an iron gate, over which was the crest of the borough, and in the corner a large pump for

The White House. From Gates

supplying the prison with water. In the centre of the front was a small casement from which the hand or glove was exhibited during the mart or fair. Behind this front tenement, which was very confined, was a paved courtyard; and behind this the prison or dungeon. In the courtyard was a remarkably fine mulberry tree; but a man having effected his escape by ascending it and reaching the roof of the adjoining house, it was cut down. The edifice was of Portland stone, and very strong and ancient, but extremely inconvenient and unwholesome. It was sold to a Mr Herman in 1805, for £1,000 and by him pulled down and the present house or hotel erected. In a large coach house behind, the original underground dungeon still exists, and is used as a coal cellar; the descent was by a trap door and iron ladder which was withdrawn at night. In this dungeon was confined the celebrated Jack the Painter.

During the existence of the old Gaol, criminals and vagrants were led through the public streets to take their trial in the old Town Hall, which was then the Sessions room.

Conditions in the White House were clearly grim. A petition dated 12 October 1714 survives from three female prisoners protesting at the conditions in which they were held. They had tried all their friends but could not raise the necessary funds to secure bail. They wrote plaintively to the magistrates:

tis hard and Cold Lying one the bords thes Long Nights and for want of [illeg.] shall be Eaten up of Vermine without wee have timly Relief and shall Meak the other prisoners in our Condicion, Ther is Torbay that is but a Criple at best and I fear she will loos al hir Limbs without your worship will with the Rest of the Gentlemen of the corte take our sad Condicion into your good thoughts to let us Have our Liberty to git our bread being hear almost Starved with Cold and hunger so hope your worship will grant our Request which favor may it pleas your worship will Never be forgotton and hope God will Reward you for the same and we shall Ever be bound to pray for your Worshipp's health and prosperity and Remain Your poor humble sarvants.

The document is signed with their mark by the three women: Penelope Williams, Mary Bomman [*sic*] and Elizabeth Wickers.

Transportation

Pressure grew on prison space in the course of the eighteenth century in Portsmouth as elsewhere. It was pressure compounded by growing opposition to a savage penal code which condemned to death anyone who stole goods valued at a shilling or more, and general agreement that imprisonment with hard labour was sufficient sanction for petty offenders. Petty offenders were therefore no longer whipped or sent to the gallows as a matter of course but sentenced to a period of imprisonment with hard labour, and to relieve the pressure on English gaols they were transported after 1718 to serve their sentences in the American colonies until the American Revolutionary War of 1775-83 put paid to that policy.

This was only a temporary setback however for on 13 May 1787 a small convoy of ships – HMS *Sirius,* the brig *Supply* and nine transports 'having on board a great number of convicts of both sexes' under the command of Captain Arthur Phillip RN, left Portsmouth bound for New South Wales to establish the first Australian penal colony. It has been calculated that between 1800 and 1853, when the last convict ship sailed for Australia, some 28,000 convicts were embarked at Portsmouth and altogether some 160,000 men, women and children were sent to Australia.

Convicts in fact became a common sight in Portsmouth. They lived in hulks in the harbour until a convict prison was constructed in Portsea in 1851-3. The stronger and more able-bodied convicts were employed on public works like the great dockyard extension of 1867-81 and the enormous barrack complex constructed to the east of the High Street in the 1880s. The young Beatrix Potter paid a brief visit to Portsmouth with her parents in 1884 and was particularly struck by the numbers of convicts at work in the town, supervised by warders on wooden platforms. Elderly residents still recall their grandparents and their generation telling them of the dreadful noise the convicts' chains made, dragging over the cobbled streets as the wretched men were marched each day from their prison to work and back.

Prison hulks

The prison hulks were ships that were no longer seaworthy. They usually had their masts reduced or removed, and it is clear from contemporary paintings and prints that an assortment of wooden buildings were usually constructed on their decks. They were introduced in the early 1770s in an effort to alleviate the pressures on prisons caused by the loss of the American colonies, although the greatest use was made of prison hulks during the French Wars between 1793 and 1815. Prison hulks were a cheap alternative to building more prisons on land. They were first used on the Thames but a number soon followed in Portsmouth and Langstone harbours. Conditions were appalling. The ships were seriously overcrowded, and with little or no ventilation - because the ports on the landward side were boarded over to deter escapees – they were very unhealthy and sickness and disease were rife.

The state of the White House, as well as growing pressures on space prompted an extensive programme of repairs to the borough gaol in the early eighteenth century during the mayoralty of William Rickman in 1742–3, and in due course a new jail was in fact built behind the High Street in Penny Street in 1805 with a purpose-built Sessions room and related office accommodation. It was enlarged in 1843 and replaced itself in due course by a new prison building at Milton designed on Benthamite principles which allowed a centrally placed observer to survey all the inmates as the prison wings radiated out from this central position. It was opened in 1877.

The town was badly treated over this project. While the new prison was still in course of construction, the Prisons Act came into force. All local gaols were transferred to the control of central government which claimed not only the old gaol but the new one under construction. The government surrendered their claim to the old gaol eventually but the town was saddled with the cost of the new building - £40,000 – and until 1924 was paying about £1,400 a year in interest and the repayment of capital.

Today

Sessions and Assizes were abolished in 1971. Sessions Courts were replaced by Magistrates Courts and today Portsmouth Magistrates Court in Winston Churchill Avenue deals with most criminal cases. In fact over 95 per cent of criminal cases start in these courts. Crown Courts replaced the Assizes and the Portsmouth Crown Court, which sits alongside the Magistrates Court in the nearby Courts of Justice, also in Winston Churchill Avenue, deals with more serious criminal cases, just as the

Assizes did, such as murder, rape or robberies, some of which are on appeal or referred there from the Magistrates Court.

The essential business of these modern courts is still part of a process which our medieval forbears would understand and be all too familiar with. That process has been refined considerably over the centuries, and the volume of business has increased exponentially but it is still one based on an understanding that we are still responsible for each other's behaviour and if any individual is suspected of a crime or misdemeanour it is the duty of his neighbours – albeit through a series of different agencies nowadays – to produce that miscreant in court.

CHAPTER 13

A 'Deed of Horror'
1829

*This town was, on Monday morning, thrown into a state of
frightful consternation, by the discovery of as appalling a deed
of horror, as any yet unfolded in the annals of crime of this or
any other country and one far more atrocious than any before
perpetrated in this town... .*

Thus the *Hampshire Telegraph* opened its report on the
discovery of the bodies of Mr Samuel Langtrey and
his housekeeper, Mrs Charity Joliffe, in Mr
Langtrey's house in Prospect Row on 2 March 1829.
Mr Langtrey was a retired bricklayer. He was nearly eighty years
old and an invalid. Mrs Joliffe was sixty years old and a distant
relative. Prospect Row stood where Gunwharf Road lies today. It
formed a thoroughfare from Lombard Street, inside the old town
walls, to Portsea. The fortifications were still in place in 1829 and
the roadway was much narrower than it is today with a high
rampart bounding it on the west. There were a number of public
houses in the street and by the time the fortifications came down
in the 1880s the area did not enjoy a good reputation but it was
still a respectable neighbourhood in the 1820s.

*An early nineteenth century perspective looking towards Prospect Row and the
lane from Portsmouth to Portsea.* From Gates

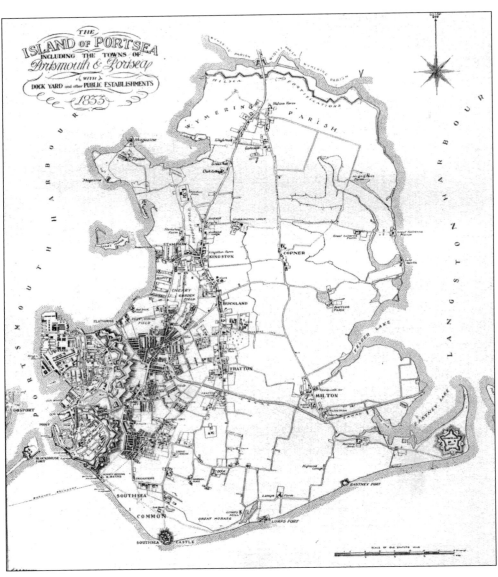

Portsmouth in 1833. From Gates

Mr Langtrey and Mrs Joliffe were the only occupants of the house that night. There were no signs of life the following morning and it was not long before their neighbours became curious and in due course, suspicious. A man managed to get into the building and there he discovered the body of Mrs Joliffe lying on the floor. A constable was hurriedly sent for. It was not a pretty sight. Mrs Joliffe had been killed by blows from a slater's hammer which was found on the premises covered with blood, and wounds which had been inflicted with a knife which could not be found. Her head was practically severed from her body.

Upstairs they found the body of Mr Langtrey. He had also been attacked with the hammer and his throat had been cut. Over £600 had been taken from a chest. The case created a sensation in the town and every detail was recounted by the local newspapers to an avid readership. The funeral took place a week after the gruesome discoveries. It was described as a 'melancholy spectacle'. The victims were buried in St Thomas's Churchyard in one grave. The event 'attracted an immense concourse of persons, and excited feelings of the strongest commiseration for their unhappy fate'.

> *The funeral took place about eleven o'clock. The bodies were conveyed in two hearses, four coaches followed, and a post coach closed the procession with the medical gentlemen who were called into attendance at the Coroner's Inquest.*

A pardon was promised to any accomplice who disclosed the identity of the culprit, and a reward of £200 was promised for information which led to the conviction of those responsible for the crime. Local police officers, assisted by Mr Bishop 'the Bow Street Officer', pursued the case enthusiastically.

Remarkably, the *Hampshire Telegraph* was able to announce, within a fortnight of the first details of the atrocity emerging, that John Stacey and his father had been apprehended and charged. It would emerge in due course that Stacey was a young man who by the nature of his trade was not unknown within the community, which only added to the general shock and horror. Meanwhile the paper intoned:

> *It will relieve the public mind to learn that the monster who perpetrated these bloody deeds is no longer at large. By the indefatigable exertions of the excellent and highly respected Chief Magistrate of this Borough (Edward Carter Esq.), and*

the activity of Mr Edward Hunt, and the other Officers of our police, the villain has not only been apprehended, but so complete a chain of evidence has been obtained to substantiate this horrible charge against him, as to render an escape from punishment impossible.

The paper also reported 'with astonishment' that Stacey was present in the crowd at the funeral:

that it is ascertained by what has transpired since the appre-hension of the murderer, that the villain himself was during some part of the time among the spectators on this sad occasion, but that the scene so overcame him, he retired from it, and had recourse to the use of spirits.

As the *Hampshire Telegraph* claimed, the 'chain of evidence' was indeed very damning. It seems that shortly after the victims' funerals Stacey, who was described as twenty years of age and an out-door apprentice of Mr Weeks, one of the constables, and a hair-dresser in Warblington Street, was seen going into the country in an open chaise with two girls 'of bad character'. His wages were only two shillings and six pence a week 'which would not allow of such proceedings'. He was suspected immediately. Mr Weeks was approached. He informed the inquirers that as Stacey had a swelling on his hand he had not been able to work for several days. As for the excursion in the chaise, 'he could not account for any means Stacey had of incurring such an expense'.

Mr Hunt, with two assistants drawn from amongst the constables, including Mr Weeks, Stacey's employer, therefore set off in pursuit of Stacey leaving other members of his team, Lewis, Way and Serjeant, in Portsmouth to look for evidence which might implicate Stacey. The suspect was traced to a house in Portchester where he was apprehended with the two girls, Ann Hawkins and Sarah Harris. He reportedly exclaimed on seeing Mr Hunt, 'I am done.' All three were brought back to Portsmouth and taken straight to the town gaol where questioning began immediately before the Mayor, although it was by this time early evening. The questioning continued until a late hour.

The *Hampshire Telegraph* detailed the case against Stacey. Apparently the prisoner, as he now was, went every Saturday to shave Langtrey. There he 'had frequent conversations with him' and, more ominously, 'was acquainted with every part of the house'. On the Saturday before the murder he shaved the old man and promised to bring him a copy of a pamphlet called the *Book of Martyrs.* On Sunday, after dinner, the day of the murder, he came into Portsmouth with a youth called Connoymore who was apprenticed to his brother-in-law, Linnet, who was actually a constable in Portsea. They spent the night at Linnet's house. It was Connoymore who was sent to purchase the copy of the pamphlet. Stacey asked Connoymore to pay for it himself as he, Stacey, had no money but he promised that he would reimburse him the sixpence another time. The book was bought and the two men, Stacey and Connoymore, set off for Stacey's father's home at Halfway-houses, which is roughly where Landport is today. The area was known as Halfway-houses as it was reckoned, originally, to be halfway between the town of Portsea and the parish church of St Mary's at Kingston.

They both remained there until about twenty minutes before six o'clock when Stacey left alone. He returned just over two hours later at eight o'clock 'agitated and flurried', and disappeared hurriedly upstairs. He called his father to join him and they remained there, upstairs, nearly half-an-hour. When they came down Connoymore reported that Stacey went into the yard and washed himself. The father then sent Connoymore to Portsea to buy bread and cheese, although both could have been obtained at a shop nearby. When Connoymore returned with his purchases Stacey was sitting by the fire without his shirt which was drying before the heat. When it was dry, Stacey put it on again and he and Connymore returned to Stacey's brother-in-law's, Linnet's, house where they spent the night.

When they got there Connymore commented that Stacey's clothes seemed to be 'much blooded'. Stacey said that he had been in a fight and that his nose had bled copiously. The clothes were so very bloody though that Connymore reported

that it was necessary to scrape them with a knife – although the shirt had been washed; when his coat was pulled off, blood was on the wristbands – the inside of his shoes were also very bloody.

Stacey apparently went to work every day after the murder until the Thursday morning when he complained of having a bad hand

since which time he got into bad company, and expended a great deal of money, in the purchase of seals, a watch &c – When buying these he was observ'd to have a large quantity of gold.

More incriminating evidence was coming to light elsewhere. The fellow glove to one found near the body of the housekeeper was discovered in the moats at Portsea, in a bag with a *Book of Martyrs*, 'the prisoner taking the latter, it is supposed, as a pretext for gaining admission into the deceased's house'. There were 'various other circumstances connected with the prisoner', reported the *Hampshire Telegraph*, 'which leave no doubt of his guilt'. A large clasp knife had been found under the Lion Gate footbridge in Portsea by a convict called John Woodward who was employed on public works under way there. It was very bloody apparently, and had some hair attached to it. It was a strong knife, very broad, three inches long with a horn handle four inches long 'with a square top somewhat inclining forward'. Stacey admitted that it was his. He had also remarked some time since that he knew Langtrey had £600.

The paper also reported that Stacey had come up with a somewhat far-fetched tale to the effect that on the night of the murder he met someone in Camden Alley who agreed with him to commit the crime. When they arrived at the Quay Gates they tossed up which of the two of them would commit the deed; his associate lost. They exchanged clothes, the other man repaired to Mr Langtrey's house and did the awful deed. When they met up, they again exchanged clothes and the money was handed over to the prisoner. The *Hampshire Telegraph* clearly did not believe a word of this. It did report however that when Stacey was apprehended there was no money on him and that he had continued to work from the Monday after the murder until the following Thursday, and in that time he shaved many people including Mr Bishop, the Bow Street officer

and as the mind of every one was engrossed by the murders, many remarks on it were made to Stacey, particularly by one person, who observed, in joke, that perhaps among the many examined 'probably you, John, will be taken up next';

He was not observed however to be the least moved by this shaft of wit but on another occasion, when he was shaving a man, it was remarked that a clue had been found to the murderer and 'he was now observed to be agitated, and cut the person's chin, who rebuked him for it, but still there was no suspicion of him'.

His father had been apprehended on suspicion of being concerned with the murder and would, said the *Hampshire*

Telegraph, 'be committed as an accessory after the fact'. The paper had learnt that the old man was considerably troubled, claiming in a conversation with the turnkey, Mr Hill, to have been visited in the night by someone dressed like a gentleman with a white neck handkerchief who had urged him to tell the truth. Mr Hill reported this to the Mayor who repaired himself to the cell to hear what old Mr Stacey had to say.

He admitted that his son came home on the Sunday evening at about eight o'clock, and that when he went upstairs, he followed him. His son threw a bag of money on the bed. He asked him how he had come by it, and why his clothing was covered in blood. Stacey persisted that he had been involved in a fight but he refused to say how he had come by the money. He admitted finally a few days later that he had murdered Mr Langtrey and his housekeeper in order to obtain the money. Old Mr Stacey said that he counted the money when his son first brought it into the house. There was £630. They hid it initially in a dung-heap at the back of the house. Later the older man removed the money from there and buried it in a spot at Copnor. He was taken to the alleged burial place by the authorities and there they discovered, wrapped in a silk hand-kerchief, the sum of £627, principally in notes, and the watch which the culprit had purchased.

With some satisfaction, the *Hampshire Telegraph* reported in due course that, although Mr Bishop, the Bow Street officer, was in the town at the time, he had no share in the prisoner's apprehension. It was a triumph for local powers of detection. It could even have been described by the rueful London man as a close shave!

Lion Gate. It pierced the Portsea fortifications at the upper end of Queen Street. It was built in 1777, taken down in 1871 and re-erected at the Naval Barracks in Edinburgh Road. From Gates

CHAPTER 14

The Blossom Alley Murder
1923

On 26 January 1923 a woman called Mary Pelham, a prostitute who was also known as 'Brighton Mary', was bludgeoned to death in a tumble-down house in Blossom Alley in Portsea. Blossom Alley ran between North Street and Cross Street. Apparently Mary lived alone in the house with her cat. The house consisted of three rooms, one above the other, connected by a winding staircase. She was only thirty-eight and at one time she sold matches and flowers on the streets. She was last seen alive the previous evening when she went to an eating house in Queen Street known as the *Live and Let Live*. There she presented a basin and asked for some mash, purportedly for her cat but perhaps more likely for herself. She was seen later that evening with a sailor.

It had not been an easy twelve months for the Borough Police or, for that matter, for the people of Portsea. Barely six months before, in July 1922, a young child, three-year old Georgie Smith, had gone missing while playing in the street outside his grandmother's house. A medium was even brought in to try and trace the child but it was not until September 1922 that James Kerrigan of 55, Orange Street, a widower, went up into his attic to look for something, and discovered there more than he could possibly have bargained for. In a trunk in his attic, bound with rope, he found the body of 'Wee Georgie', as he was known to his family and friends. Extraordinarily and very sadly, it emerged that Georgie had been abducted by James Kerrigan's teenage son, Leonard, while he was suffering from an epileptic seizure. He had bound the baby with rope and placed him in the box while he was probably still alive. Leonard was subsequently sentenced to be detained in an institution for the insane.

As if that was not misery enough for the local population, they had to contend now with another tragedy in their midst, although for the children it was clearly an exciting departure from their usual humdrum existence. One elderly lady recalled when asked what she could remember of the Blossom Alley murder that 'day after day, we children crowded around the house, looking for I don't know what'.

Detectives from Scotland Yard were brought in to assist the borough police with this new investigation. Allegedly Mary had been strangled and battered to death with a beer bottle. A huge identification parade was held at the Naval Barracks in the hope that those who saw her with the sailor on the night she was last seen might be able to pick the man out. Three thousand five hundred men were assembled on the parade ground. But it was to no avail. Although it was reported that a sailor was identified, there was presumably not enough evidence to bring charges and the crime was never solved officially.

However, the case created a sensation both locally and nationally, not, sadly, because of the manner of Mary's death, but because of the circumstances in which she lived and died. There was a public outcry. She was in fact found in a room which measured ten feet four inches by five feet two inches, and the height of the ceiling varied between nine feet ten inches and six feet eight inches because of the collapsing floors and ceilings.

The *Hampshire Telegraph* was deeply shocked. A few weeks later it published a special feature on Portsmouth's slum areas. The conditions, it declared, under which many Portsmouth people lived, were worse than the worst of London's slums. It also quoted 'an official' 'whose duties have carried him into the backwaters of all the large towns in England'. He assured the paper that

> *Portsmouth, as far as its slums were concerned, was comparable only with the big industrial towns of the North, where there was serious congestion and overcrowding in tumble-down and unhealthy houses, built in such close proximity that there was barely air space.... How many are there in Portsmouth, apart from those compelled by force of circumstances to live their days in the squalid surroundings of our slums, who have the faintest conception of the deplorable state of affairs that exist?*

Blossom Alley was described in the report as 'a depressing passage, the opposite walls of which can be almost touched by extending the arms' and with its nineteen houses and the five courts leading out of it, it was, said the author of the report, like many similarly dreary and overcrowded thoroughfares in the neighbourhood. Portsea had not always been like this though. This suburb of the original walled town of Portsmouth developed in the early eighteenth century to accommodate the town's growing population. Building began outside the town walls to the north, on Portsmouth Common, and on the East and West Dock Fields which were part of the ancient common-field system of the original settlement. The new suburb developed rapidly. Daniel Defoe noted when he visited Portsmouth in 1724 that 'since the encrease of business at this place, by the long continuance of the war'

> the confluence of people has been so great, and the town not admitting any enlargement for buildings, that a kind of suburb or rather a new town has been built on the healthy ground adjoining to the town, which is so well built, and seems to encrease so fast, that in time it threatens to outdo for numbers of inhabitants, and beauty of buildings, even the town itself.

And indeed, by the end of the eighteenth century, Portsea, as the new suburb was now known, was three times as large as Portsmouth. When the first census took place in 1801, the population of the parish of Portsmouth was 7,839 and that of the parish of Portsea, 24,327. The population grew rapidly during the nineteenth century, more than doubling every fifty years from 32,166 in 1801 to 72,096 in 1851 and 190,281 in 1901. Such rapid growth put particular pressure on the older areas of the town and, as the original beautiful and well-built houses in Portsea were divided and sub-divided to accommodate the newcomers, and a warren of courts and alleyways absorbed the stabling, outhouses and gardens of the old properties, so increasing public health problems culminated in devastating outbreaks of cholera in 1848 and 1849.

The report which was published eventually on the outbreaks was not comfortable reading. They were due, the writers said, to 'ill-paved and uncleansed streets, imperfect privy accommodation, crowded courts and houses, with large exposed middens and cesspools; and no adequate power for effective local government'. Further, the report said, the excess of disease was distinctly traceable to undrained and crowded districts, to deficient ventilation, to the absence of a full water-supply and of sewers and drains generally. It was a damning indictment of the failure of the borough council and of those in charge at that time

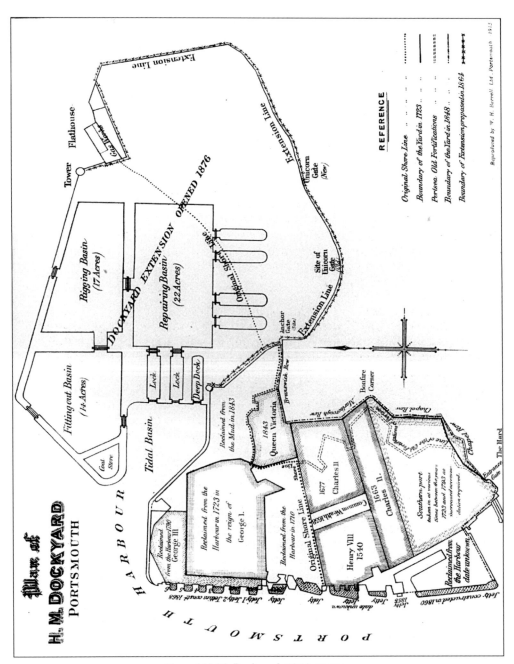

Plan of H.M. Dockyard, 1913. PMRS

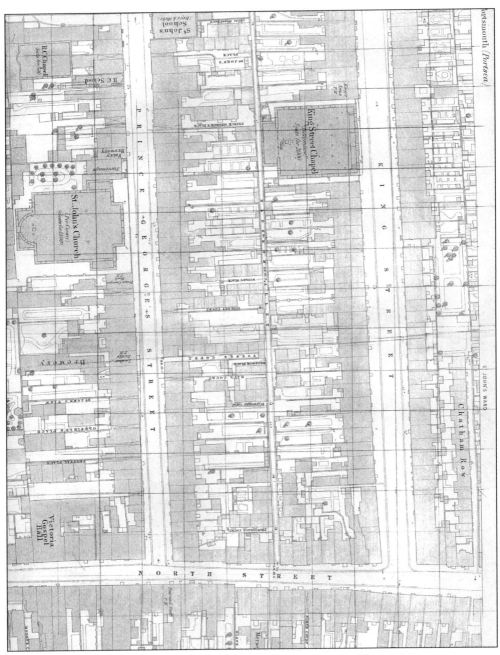

Blossom Alley from the 1861 1:500 10.56 feet to One Statute Mile O.S. Map. PMES

of cleansing, paving and lighting, to get to grips with the problems of unregulated development.

Mary Pelham's sad death in her small squalid room in Blossom Alley showed that very little changed in the ensuing half century. This is particularly clear in the fascinating set of interviews with former residents of the area which James Cramer, Portsmouth's police historian, undertook when he began a significant piece of research in 1975 into housing and social conditions generally in Portsea between 1919 and 1939.

A number of those he interviewed spoke of the neighbourhood's former and now faded glories – of the grand houses with large gardens, stable yards and coach houses. King Street, said one elderly gentleman, was rather a nice street 'although surrounded by rather more dubious property'. His own childhood home, he recalled

> *was a fairly large house and stone steps led up to the front door which his grandmother used to whiten with hearth-stone. Two stone columns supported the porch and the front room on the first floor was big enough for a club-room. There were two big cellars with fireplaces and a coal cellar big enough to hold ten tons of coal.... The kitchen had a large range with, he thought, two ovens and he remembers the two big black iron kettles which always stood on top of the range.*

Blossom Alley was next to King Street and 'there was generally a row going on in one of the houses, and to see a drunk lying in the gutter was nothing unusual, or a street fight'. Two of the biggest houses in King Street, he said, were occupied by a Royal Naval commander, and a Miss Allsop 'who were much looked up to so I suppose that gave a bit of "tone" to the street'.

Senior naval officers and dockyard officials, and wealthy merchants and tradesmen occupied all the considerable properties in Portsea at one time. Another of James Cramer's interviewees once lived at 76 Prince George Street and described what was clearly a magnificent property. The house was enormous with four floors, a basement and attics and the former tenants recalled fondly 'lovely views from the top floor', the wide spiral stairs and an inside bathroom and lavatory. There was also a wide flight of steps leading up to the front door and a generously proportioned entrance hall, and there were still chandeliers in some of the rooms. Blossom Alley was at the back of the house but those living in Prince George Street in 1926

The *Coal Exchange* in Cross Street in 1894. From Gates

Dwelling houses in Cross Street in 1894. From Gates

claimed that they were not over-bothered by their neighbours. Those neighbours certainly enjoyed the glimpses they had of other people's lives. One elderly lady often walked through Blossom Alley with her friends who lived nearby. She said she liked going through all the backways during her childhood because she could see the trees in the back gardens, particularly from Blossom Alley.

Sister Ethel Shepherdson, who came to Portsmouth in 1925 to be Superintendent-in-charge of St Paul's Home for Girls which was run by the Free Church Women's Council, recalled with fondness their property which stood on the corner of King Street and North Street. It was still a fine building. The Home had occupied the building since 1908. Before then it had been occupied by a tally-man who sold bales of cloth and before him it had belonged to a doctor. 'It was a beautiful house,' she said, 'with a double front door at the top of three steps with a central hall, a wide staircase with mahogany banisters, and a statue of a lady holding a lamp, with a balcony at the top'. Steps led from the entrance hall to the kitchen, sculleries and other domestic offices below stairs. The reception rooms on the ground floor were huge and there was one long and very grand room on the first floor which must have been the original drawing-room.

She recalled that there was a 'tremendous' amount of poverty all around

> *but King Street (as were some other streets) was a mixture of beautiful houses occupied by well-to-do people, and small one-up-and-one-down houses in terraces, or large houses which had been occupied by better-off families who had moved out, allowing a lot of poorer people to live in their place.*

She remembered particularly a large house in Havant Street which belonged to Winchester College. When the family which lived there moved out, a lot of tenants and sub-tenants moved in, and beds were let at a shilling a night. The place was verminous and she was very surprised that such a body could thus profit from the poverty of so many people. Many other people in fact profited from such poverty. Winchester College, as an institution, was something of an exception to the rule. The bulk of the absentee landlords were actually ordinary Portsmouth men and women who owned a few properties and lived off the rents, especially in their old age. State and occupational pensions are very much twentieth century developments.

Some of these landlords were in fact very respectable members of the local community. Many of them seem to have been local shopkeepers and businessmen. However, one of James Cramer's interviewees recalled that Miss, later Dame, Elizabeth Kelly, who was appointed Portsmouth's first lady magistrate in 1920, owned courts off Queen Street where local prostitutes plied their trade.

The accounts of the conditions in which some families lived are grim:

> *the house was very old, with a bay window, and was 'condemned'. There was a basement but it was never used, as it was blocked off for some reason. On the ground floor there was a small sitting-room, where the family did their cooking. Two families shared the outside toilet and wash-house. Above the sitting-room was one bedroom and above that was another but this could not be used as the roof was dangerous...*
>
> *All the houses in which [the family] lived in Portsea were infested with bugs, but these came from the walls and defied all efforts to remove them. There were courts in Hawke Street, little houses, with one room up and one down – with shared taps and toilets. Corporation used to send men with long rubber boots to clean and fumigate the outside toilets, pick up dead dogs from streets, and so on.*
>
> *The house [in Cross Street] had no sink, water or lavatory. The waste was emptied into a hole in the ground of the cellar.*

Sister Ethel remembered being called to a house in Blossom Alley when she first came to the town in 1925:

> *I stepped down into a living room, with no windows, lit by a candle in a bottle. A baby was in convulsions – the parents had no bath or large receptacle and no supply of water available for heating. The doctor was called – when he came he did not enter the house but said 'Give it some castor oil'. I told him that the baby was unconscious and he said 'Give it some oil when it comes to, then. That will be seven-and-sixpence'. Although the baby's father only earned about 30s. a week he paid the fee and I believe that I reimbursed him later. I managed to get some hot water and cold pads and the child recovered later.*

Blossom Alley was out of bounds, she said, to the Navy after the murder in 1923

and people were horrified when they learned that I had gone there at night. People were frightened to enter the area but the people who lived there were always so friendly and appreciated what one did to help them.

It was a society which was bolstered by a whole series of lifelines: the Salvation Army which amongst many other things supplied slum children with farthing breakfasts; assorted Naval charities and a number of boot funds; soup kitchens; junk sold in gutters round the dockyard walls; the pawnbroker's shop in Cross Street; grocers who gave food on credit to prevent a family of children starving, compassionate teachers in local schools who would supply clothing; and the many initiatives of different men and women in the town such as PC Tilbury, the local policeman who collected money at Fratton Park to buy stale bread and cakes at the end of the day from bakers for the children of poor families in Portsea. There was also the *Live and Let Live* in Queen Street where Mary Pelham was seen on the night she died which provided penny dinners which consisted of 'a halfpennyworth of pudding soaked in gravy, and another halfpennyworth of some kind of pudding with jam on it'.

The alternative was the harrowing experience of the workhouse where at least one of James Cramer's interviewees, a woman, spent time. She wrote:

I was in St Mary's Workhouse for ten months about 1929. We had five children, my husband had left me. I was living in Charlotte Street then. I had no money for food or rent so I went to the Parish Relief people in St Michael's Road. They sent my children to a separate part of the Workhouse and I worked in the workhouse laundry. The conditions were terrible. For breakfast there was unsweetened porridge, the dinners were small, and there was bread and butter for tea (with jam extra on Saturdays). We had no dinners on Saturdays except for bread and cheese. One of my children died in the workhouse, ten months old, from convulsions; one invalid daughter was sent to Nazareth House, and two girls went to a convent in Somerset. The five-year-old boy stayed with me when the church got me a job with the Arnett family.

St Paul's Home for Girls was a significant lifeline. The police or anybody finding a homeless girl would bring her to their shelter which occupied the former stable accommodation. The shelter provided sleeping accommodation in wooden partitioned cubicles. After time spent in the shelter a girl would be allowed into the home in the main building. Sister Ethel explained to James Cramer that this was because there was so much scabies, verminous infestation and venereal disease prevalent that they did not want to make conditions worse among the girls already occupying the main house. There they were charged sixpence for bed and breakfast but the rate was waived if the girl had no money. Girls who had tried to commit suicide were also brought to the shelter.

Sister Ethel was also an honorary probation officer. She attended court every day and made herself responsible for girls brought before the court on occasion. If girls were found wandering around the town she would try and make arrangements for them to travel back to their home towns after inquiries had been made. It was known, she said, for prostitutes to hang around the railway stations and recruit likely-looking young girls arriving in the town.

Was Mary Pelham recruited to be a prostitute at the Town Station or at the Harbour? Reports in the local papers said that she came from the North of England, that she married Herman Pelham whom she met in domestic service in Sunderland. When her husband went to war, she apparently came south, first to Brighton and then to Portsmouth, where she set up home at 14 Blossom Alley. Apparently when Herman returned from the war he knew already that she was working as a prostitute but was so dismayed by the squalor of the life she was leading that he abandoned her.

There is another possibility that she might be the Mary Pelham who is listed in the 1891 Census aged eight living with her parents, brother and two sisters at Blatchington near Seaford, which is near enough Brighton for her to have earned the nickname of 'Brighton Mary' when she came to ply her trade as a prostitute in Portsmouth, recruited perhaps at one of Portsmouth's railway stations.

She was reportedly a good neighbour and did what she could when she was able to do so to help those who lived alongside her, especially children. This is in fact a feature of all the accounts of life in Portsea between the two world wars. What little you had, you often shared with your neighbours. Mary was also described as 'a mother of the matelots'. She would hide men who were too drunk to make their own way back to their ships or to barracks, to save them from the wrath and harsh discipline of the naval patrols.

On the night she died she was seen arm-in-arm with a sailor heading for home. She was seen some fifteen minutes later in Queen Street at the *Live and Let Live*, where she said that she was in a hurry as she had to get some chips for her 'chap'. The next morning her neighbour, Mary Riley, was passing 14 Blossom Alley and noticed that the door was open. She called out but there was no answer. She went in and climbed the stairs to the bedroom. She opened the door and Mary lay there, the victim of a savage attack. Around her head and shoulders, the reports said

> *the bedclothes were dark and in a sticky mass of blood. A gash from Mary Pelham's forehead to the top of her nose, glistened in the light. Tied in a half-hitch around her neck was a light blue handkerchief or scarf. On the bed, the shattered parts of a pint oat malt stout bottle.*

Following a tip-off, police inquiries focussed on a sailor on board the battleship *Ramillies*. He was taken in for questioning but he was never formally arrested and charged with the crime, nor was his name ever released. The Borough Police might not have been able to find Mary Pelham's killer but her death galvanised the Borough Council into tackling more seriously the whole issue of slum clearance and housing provision generally. The figures speak for themselves: 27 new houses built in 1922, 162 in 1923, 221 in 1924, 421 in 1925, 682 in 1926 and 898 in 1927. Finally, in 1929, a start was made with the council's scheme to erect small dwellings to be used for the re-housing of tenants from the Portsea area dispossessed when their houses were condemned under the council's Slum Clearance Scheme. Contracts started during the year for the erection of 216 houses on the Hilsea housing site and 153 houses and twelve flats on the Eastern Road. A number of James Cramer's interviewees and correspondents were actually rehoused on these particular sites.

CHAPTER 15

Sherlock Holmes, Dr Watson – and Southsea!
1882–1890

On the night of 10-11 January 1941 Portsmouth was given a 'hammering' from the air. It was claimed afterwards that the German raiders were led by a pilot who was acquainted with the city. Whether he was or not, large parts of the city were destroyed including the main shopping centres in Palmerston Road, King's Road and Commercial Road, and a host of key buildings: the Guildhall, six churches, the Eye and Ear Hospital, part of the Royal Hospital, Clarence Pier, the Hippodrome and three cinemas, the Dockyard School, the Connaught Drill Hall, the Central Hotel, the Royal Sailors' Rest, and the Salvation Army Citadel in Lake Road. Over 25,000 incendiaries were dropped as well as HE (High Explosive) bombs. At one time over twenty-eight major fires raged with no effective supplies of water to fight the flames, as the water mains had been fractured.

The Lord Mayor, then Mr DL Daley (he was knighted later in the war), rallied his fellow-citizens the following day in the pages of the *Evening News*. He congratulated them on the courage they had displayed in the face of such an onslaught, and he thanked the public services, particularly the fire fighting services, for their tireless efforts to save the city. He concluded his remarks with positively Churchillian rhetoric:

We are bruised, but we are not daunted, and we are still as determined as ever to stand side by side with other cities who have felt the blast of the enemy, and we shall with them, persevere with an unflagging spirit towards a conclusive and decisive victory.

To you all, therefore, I say what I feel you would wish me to say – keep a stout heart, keep your chins firm and your heads high. Be calm, be steadfast, be firm.

He was asking a lot. Many had lost all their worldly goods and

Kings Road and Elm Grove in 1943. The wreckage of Bush Villas lay to the right of the Elm Grove Baptist Church. PMRS

were homeless. Nelson's Portsmouth of elegant Georgian streets, shops and coaching inns had been destroyed, as well as great swathes of small houses built in the course of the nineteenth century outside the old town in Portsea, Landport and Buckland to house dockyard workers. Outside the dockyard itself, which survived remarkably unscathed due to the diligence of the many batteries of anti-aircraft guns, much of Portsmouth's heritage of historic buildings, those associated with key events and famous people in its history, was lost forever. They included 1 Bush Villas, Elm Grove, Southsea, where Dr Arthur Conan Doyle put up his brass plate in 1882 and where, in due course, the most famous duo in detective fiction would be created: Sherlock Holmes and Dr Watson.

By assiduous study of shipping movements, it has been calculated by Geoffrey Stavert, author of *A Study in Southsea*, that young Dr Doyle arrived in Portsmouth on Saturday 24 June 1882 by steamer from Plymouth, and disembarked at Clarence Pier. An Irish Catholic, Conan Doyle was born and brought up in Scotland. He qualified at Edinburgh University Medical School in 1881.

Between qualifying and arriving in Southsea he had tried his hand as a ship's doctor but this had not been a great success. He had fallen ill. He gained useful experience however, once he had

Clarence Pier where Conan Doyle landed on his arrival in Portsmouth in June 1882. PMRS

recovered, in busy practices in Sheffield and Birmingham and then, in Plymouth. He had great hopes of a partnership there but things did not work out. When his efforts to obtain a position in Tavistock came to nothing, he packed his bags, obtained a ticket and embarked on an Irish steamer to seek his fortune elsewhere. He got off at the first port of call – Portsmouth.

He probably secured lodgings in or near Highbury Street in the old town of Portsmouth, only a short walk from the landing stage at Clarence Pier. He had determined now to set up his own medical practice. He had to establish first where the pre-existing practices were situated and once that was clear, where exactly any windows of opportunity might exist. He had then to seek out a set of suitable – and cheap – premises. No. 1, Bush Villas, Elm Grove, next door to the Elm Grove Baptist Church, suited admirably and by 1 July 1882 he was in business.

Elm Grove was a good choice. It was on the northern boundary of fashionable Southsea where there were already fourteen doctors in practice – four of them in fact in nearby Kent Road. Elm Grove was also adjacent to King's Road, which was a busy shopping street where he might expect to attract passing trade. More importantly however, to the north of Elm Grove were the densely-populated streets of Somers Town, inhabited by skilled dockyard workers and their families, and to the west was Croxton Town, a chequerboard of narrow and not

"BUSH HOTEL"

King's Road, Southsea.

COMMERCIAL AND FAMILY HOTEL.

WINES AND SPIRITS of the Choicest Kinds

Bass & Allsopp's Ales,
On Draught and in Bottles.

Proprietor - E. H. HILL.

The Largest Billiard Saloon in the Town.

Tables by Burroughs and Watts.

Head Quarters of the Cyclist's Touring Club.
SOUTHSEA.

An advertisement for the Bush Hotel *which stood next door to Nos. 1 and 2 Bush Villas. They can be made out between the Baptist Church and the hotel.* PMRS

A sunny afternoon in Elm Grove, c.1890. PMRS

The shops of Kings Road, c. 1890. PMRS

particularly healthy streets.

It was in these streets that he hoped he would find sufficient business, not only to maintain his own household, but also to allow him to remit funds to his mother in Edinburgh. It was not easy. At the beginning he had no assistance whatsoever. He received his patients himself, dealt with their medical problems, prescribed and made up their medicines when necessary and, under cover of darkness, polished his own brass plate and then cooked his supper.

Geoffrey Stavert believes that at this time Conan Doyle was not above a little self-publicity in the interests of advancing his business. In early November there was an accident in the street outside his surgery. He rushed out to give assistance - and went out again shortly afterwards to file a short account of what had happened at the *Evening News* office. The report appeared later that same day:

> *Accident in Elm Grove. An accident, which might have led to serious consequences, occurred this afternoon in Elm Grove. As Mr Robinson, of Victoria Road, was riding in front of the Bush Hotel, his stirrup leather snapped and he was thrown to the ground, the animal rearing at the same time and falling partially upon him. He was conveyed into the house of Dr Conan Doyle, of Bush Villas, and that gentleman was able to pronounce that, though considerably shaken and bruised, there was no injury of any consequence.*

There is another, almost certainly unsolicited, report in the *Evening News* on 27 September 1884:

> *Accident in Southsea. About 12 o'clock on Monday, one of the employees of Mr Burton, St Paul's Square, was accidentally stabbed by one of his companions. The wound penetrated through the side, and narrowly escaped dividing the lung. The sufferer was conveyed to his house by Dr Conan Doyle of Southsea, who dressed his wound, and he is now understood to be doing well.*

Conan Doyle was an assiduous reader of the *Evening News*. He went out each evening to Miss Gunning's shop in Elm Grove to buy his copy. Its closely-printed pages were packed with a tantalising mix of local, national and international stories, reports from the law courts, shipping movements, advertise-

ments and personal columns. Many of the ingredients of Conan
Doyle's novels were collected during his Portsmouth years and
the *Evening News* played no small part in supplying material.
Eagle-eyed Geoffrey Stavert noted in a story in the *Evening
News* that a Chief Inspector Sherlock of B division was in court
in Westminster on 4 January 1883, watching a case on behalf of
the police which had involved a brawl at the Anchor Inn, York
Street, Westminster. Did Conan Doyle squirrel away this
unusual name at this time, and resurrect it in due course when
he was casting around for a name for his fictional detective?

By the end of 1882 Conan Doyle had sufficient patients to
allow his younger brother, Innes, who was still of school age to
join him. In due course the boy went to the Portsmouth
Grammar School. There was also enough money now to
employ a housekeeper who willingly undertook the job of recep-
tionist and may well, in her turn, have provided inspiration for
Holmes and Watson's landlady at 221B Baker Street, Mrs
Hudson. The new housekeeper was a treasure. She clearly
appreciated the situation quickly and played a useful role,
making patients wait quite unnecessarily and fixing appointments at very specific times, thus creating the impression that
the doctor was a particularly busy man. With his practice
launched, Conan Doyle could afford now to embrace local
society, which he did with enthusiasm.

He was introduced to the local sporting fraternity by his near
neighbour, Dr William Pike, who lived at Yarborough Villa, at
the top of Yarborough Road, on the other side of the Elm Grove
Baptist Church. He reportedly enjoyed a game of bowls and
probably introduced Conan Doyle to the Southsea Bowling
Club where the latter became a keen player. Another doctor, Dr
Robert Weston who practised in North End, introduced him to
local cricketing circles and Conan Doyle played for the North
End Cricket Club, which in due course changed its name to the
Portsmouth Cricket Club, to considerable acclaim for most of
the time he was living in Portsmouth. He was also a founder-
member of the Portsmouth football club where, under the
thinly-veiled disguise of the name AC Smith, he distinguished
himself on a number of occasions in goal. Dr Pike in due course
was reincarnated as Dr Porter in *The Stark Munro Letters*.

The practice grew slowly however. Conan Doyle gained
some useful work as a medical referee through his friendship
with Mr George Barnden, who was the Superintendent of the
Portsmouth branch of the Gresham Insurance Company. He

was also sent patients by local dentist Mr William Kirton, but it is clear that although the practice was growing it was not growing fast enough to satisfy the energetic Dr Conan Doyle. In short, in the words of Geoffrey Stavert, 'it was far from being a full-time profession'.

Conan Doyle was a compulsive writer however with an insatiable desire to communicate. Why should he not turn his recreational pursuit into a serious money-making enterprise? If he could get his tales published in some of the popular weekly and monthly magazines, the fees would be a most welcome addition to the income from his medical practice. He had in fact had a short story published in 1879 in *Chambers Journal*. It was an adventure story about prospecting for diamonds in South Africa. He took up his pen with enthusiasm and by mid-1883 he had had about a dozen tales published, each one earning him three or four guineas.

Able now perhaps to afford the annual subscription of a guinea a year, Conan Doyle continued to forge his path through local society by joining the Portsmouth Literary and Scientific Society. Founded in 1869, the Literary and Scientific Society had a membership made up of most of the important professional men in the town. He was nominated for membership on 6 November 1883, probably by two fellow medical men: Dr Ward Cousins of Riversdale, Kent Road and Dr Claud Claremont who lived then at 59 Green Road. On 4 December Dr Arthur Conan Doyle MB CM gave his inaugural paper to an audience of over two hundred and fifty ladies and gentlemen on the subject of 'The Arctic Seas', drawing on his experiences as a ship's doctor. At the next Annual General Meeting he was voted onto the council of the Literary and Scientific Society. The society would prove to be a rich source of material for future writing projects.

Many of his new friends and acquaintances also gave their names to characters in his stories. The Reverend Henry Maxwell Egan Desmond MA FRGS, an elderly clergyman who lived at St Vincent Lodge in Kent Road and joined the Literary and Scientific Society shortly after Conan Doyle, gave his name some twenty years later in *The Hound of the Baskervilles* to James Desmond, another elderly clergyman who lived in Westmoreland and may well have been a distant heir to the Baskerville fortune. Mr WH Charpentier, the owner of the eponymous printing and bookselling business in the High Street, Portsmouth and a keen member, with Conan Doyle, of the Southsea Bowling Club, appeared early on as a minor character – as Sub-Lieutenant Arthur Charpentier RN in the very first of the Sherlock Holmes stories, *A Study in Scarlet.*

A number of his medical friends appear in his works. Dr Pike appeared as Langdale Pike, the newspaper gossip columnist, in *The Three Gables.* The Maybury brothers, both doctors: Dr Aurelius Victor Maybury who had a practice in North End, and Dr Lysander Maybury who had a surgery in Hampshire Terrace, and was also the police surgeon, appeared in several guises on different occasions. It is in fact tempting to speculate that at this stage Conan Doyle was actually keeping cuttings from the *Evening News* which related to matters which interested him, particularly if they related to criminal or police procedural matters. There is for example the report which appeared on the inquest in Portsmouth into the death of a sixteen year-old barmaid called Elizabeth Sandford. She died from congestion of the lungs. Evidence was given by Mr William Henderson Starr, a London surgeon who was acting as locum for Dr Lysander Maybury. Forty years later, Conan Doyle has Sherlock Holmes refer to an imaginary Dr Lysander Starr in *The Three Garridebs.* Earlier on, the villain in *The Engineer's Thumb* is Colonel Lysander Stark.

Most importantly, at the beginning of the winter season of the Literary and Scientific Society in 1884, a Dr James Watson MD was nominated for membership. He was a Scotsman, born in Edinburgh in 1840 where he qualified at the Medical School and went on to take his MD while a junior houseman at the Edinburgh Royal Infirmary. He spent the next eighteen years in the Far East as Medical Officer in Britain's newest and most remote consulate in southern Manchuria. He then returned to England with his wife and two children and set up in practice at 70, Palmerston Road. He read his first paper to the Literary and Scientific Society on 23 December on the subject of 'China and Its People'. Sherlock Holmes' companion was in fact Dr John, not Dr James Watson but interestingly, in *The Man With The Twisted Lip*, Watson's wife at one point actually calls him James instead of John which would seem to be evidence that it was Dr James Watson of 70, Palmerston Road, Southsea who inspired the name of the great detective's companion on so many occasions.

Another possible candidate for the honour of inspiring the character of Dr John Watson was Dr Robert Weston. He was about the same age as Conan Doyle. He had been educated at

Palmerston Road, c. 1900. PMRS

Manchester but qualified LRCP at Edinburgh in 1882, where he might well have first met Conan Doyle. He lived at Mile End and, like several of Conan Doyle's medical friends, was also in practice in North End. He was a keen and talented cricketer and played with Conan Doyle in the North End Cricket Club. He practised in Portsmouth until his death in 1928 and persuaded many of his patients that he was the inspiration.

Conan Doyle married in 1885. The wedding was announced in the *Hampshire Telegraph* on 8 August 1885:

> *DOYLE-HAWKINS. On the 6th inst, at Thornton-in-Lonsdale Parish Church, by the Rev. SR Stable, Arthur Conan Doyle MD of Bush Villas, Southsea, to Louise, youngest daughter of the late Jeremiah Hawkins Esq, of Minsterworth, Gloucestershire.*

Louise was the sister of a young man whom Dr Pike had asked Conan Doyle to look at and give a second opinion. Jack Hawkins was twenty-five and living in lodgings with his widowed mother and sister at No. 2, Queen's Gate, an apartment building at the bottom of Osborne Road. He suffered from fits which had been getting both more frequent and severe.

The agreed prognosis was poor. Jack was suffering from cerebral meningitis, at that time incurable. The fitting was becoming increasingly embarrassing too and Conan Doyle took him into his own home where he cared for him until the end. He also became better acquainted with Jack's pretty sister.

Conan Doyle became secretary of the Literary and Scientific Society in 1886. He therefore rarely missed a meeting. His time was not wasted however, for it is clear that the meetings provided him with copy for many years to come. Major-General Alfred Drayson, a distinguished soldier who had seen service in India, South Africa and Canada as well as Great Britain, and had occupied the post of Professor of Surveying and Astronomy at the Royal Military Academy, Woolwich for fifteen years, retired to Southsea. He was the author of a number of publications including several on surveying, and he was soon nominated to be a member of the Literary and Scientific Society. He gave several papers in the following years on an astronomical subject and it has been

Three photographs of the houses and apartments occupied by the wealthier residents of Southsea, c. 1900. PMRS

suggested that Conan Doyle had General Drayson in mind when he was describing the mathematical skills of his arch-criminal, Moriarty.

Early in 1884 the General gave a lecture on 'The Earth and Its Movements' in which he dwelt at some length on something he called the ecliptic, by which he meant the passage traced out in the sky by the sun over the year. Because of the earth's tilt this plane makes an angle with the plane of the Equator. This angle measures roughly 23.5 degrees and marks the limit of the sun's travels north and south of the equator, and defines the tropical latitudes and polar circles. The General referred to this as the obliquity of the ecliptic. He may have defeated many in his audience but Conan Doyle had no difficulty understanding him, and certainly filed the information away for, in *The Greek Interpreter* which was published in the *Strand Magazine* in September 1893, Sherlock Holmes and Watson had a broad-ranging conversation which moved from golf clubs 'to the obliquity of the ecliptic'.

Not long afterwards the Agent of the Chicago and Illinois Railroad gave a lecture in which he described a train journey from Chicago to Vancouver. A rapt audience this time heard tales of the Mormon country and its people, material which Conan Doyle would use very soon afterwards in his first Sherlock Holmes novel, *A Study in Scarlet*.

He himself spoke on the Scottish thinker, Thomas Carlyle, at the Literary and Scientific Society. The lecture was not particu-larly well-received but his own enthusiasm for Carlyle is translated into his novels, for he endows Holmes with a wide literary knowledge and the name of Thomas Carlyle is dropped into the detective's conversation.

The Borough Engineer, Percy Boulnois, who became a par-ticularly close friend of Conan Doyle's, spoke on 'A Few Facts about Money' in which he discussed the Bimetallic Question. This was a somewhat theoretical problem relating to the use of gold and silver as dual standards of money. In due course, Sherlock Holmes's civil servant brother, Mycroft, is discovered to be an expert on the Bimetallic Question. There was a long lecture by the Reverend H. Shaen Solly of Southampton on Medieval miracle plays in the 1887 season of lectures – and in *The Sign of Four* Sherlock Holmes speaks most knowledgeably on the subject. Occasional lectures provided inspiration too, such as the lecture by the distinguished American preacher and anti-slavery campaigner, the Reverend Henry Ward Beecher at the King Street Chapel in Portsea. Beecher, was one of Dr Watson's heroes and he kept an unframed portrait of the preacher above his desk at 221B Baker Street.

Sherlock Holmes appeared in print for the first time in November 1887, in *Beeton's Christmas Annual* in 'A Study in Scarlet' with the author's name on the title page. It sold out within a fortnight despite the fact that initially it aroused little interest either locally or nationally. Ignored by both the *Hampshire Telegraph* and the *Portmouth Times,* Conan Doyle had to wait until the *Hampshire Post* drew local readers' attention to the new publication. The *Hampshire Post* came out once a week on Fridays and was published by Messrs Mills and Sons of Palmerston Road, Southsea. On 2 December they published a first leader which was in fact the first thorough review of a Sherlock Holmes story. The detective, the *Post* writer said, was

> a *marvellous creation, and the study of him which is given at the beginning is one of the most carefully elaborated portions of the book. As a painstaking delineation of abnormal activity Holmes is far ahead of the heroes of Gaboriau and Borisgobey.*

Conan Doyle turned now to a new hero, Micah Clarke. He produced this historical novel of that name between 1887 and 1888. It is the story of a young man who finds himself on the wrong side at the time of the Monmouth rebellion. His third

The Ladies Mile, c. 1900. PMRS

book, *The Mystery of Coomber,* was the tale of a trio of eastern mystics who return from the dead to exact retribution upon a retired Army officer for a crime committed in India forty years before. He had no intention at this stage of returning to his fictional detective. An entertaining lecture by the Dean of Winchester to the Literary and Scientific Society on everyday life in the reign of Edward III, and a brief holiday in the New Forest had fired him now to tackle a medieval topic which in due course would become *The White Company.*

However, he was invited now to meet the representative of the American publishing house of Lippincott's, who was in London looking for new literary talent. They met for dinner at the Langham Hotel in Portland Place in August 1889. The other young author present was Oscar Wilde. The result of the meeting was that Wilde went away to write *The Picture of Dorian Grey* and Conan Doyle agreed to resurrect Sherlock Holmes. He would receive £100 for not less than 40,000 words, to be delivered not later than January 1890. He in fact produced the required number of words – *The Sign of Four* - in barely a month.

His income from his literary endeavours was beginning now to rival that from medicine. He was in funds from *Micah Clarke* and *The Sign of Four.* The manuscript of *The Firm of Girdlestone & Co.* which he had completed many years before but had failed to get published, had also been accepted at long last – by the Globe Newspaper Syndicate. It was serialised in due course by *The People* newspaper and then published by Chatto and Windus. A collected edition of his magazine short stories was also published now by Longmans under the title of *The Captain of the Pole Star.*

He left Portsmouth at the end of 1890 determined still to pursue a medical career but as an eye specialist now in London. He had developed a particular interest in eye work during his early days in Portsmouth, and had taken a keen interest in the work of the Eye and Ear Hospital in Pembroke Road since its foundation in 1884. The Literary and Scientific Society gave a farewell dinner in his honour at the *Grosvenor Hotel* on the corner of Western Parade. The *Hampshire Telegraph* noted presciently of Conan Doyle in its report of the evening:

He is a fine example of the healthy mind in the healthy body, entering with equal zeal into manly sports and into those exercises of the brain which seem destined to bring him fame and fortune.

W G Gates reminded his readers in *Records of the Corporation* that it was also in Portsmouth that the doctor 'commenced those excursions in the psychic realm which have brought him absolute conviction of the continuity of existence beyond the death of the physical body'. He would pursue these particular interests with ever-increasing enthusiasm following his departure from Portsmouth.

His efforts to become an eye surgeon in London failed however and he quickly abandoned this idea in favour of becoming a full-time writer. He began now devising a series of plots set around the personalities of Sherlock Holmes and Dr Watson in their lodgings at 221B Baker Street. The proposal was accepted immediately by the *Strand Magazine* and the first adventure, *A Scandal in Bohemia,* came out in July 1891. It begins enigmatically:

> *To Sherlock Holmes she is always 'the' woman. I have seldom heard him mention her under any other name. In his eyes she eclipses and predominates the whole of her sex. It was not that he felt any emotion akin to love for Irene Adler. All emotions, and that one particularly, were abhorrent to his cold, precise, but admirably balanced mind. He was, I take it, the most perfect reasoning and observing machine that the world has seen: but, as a lover, he would have placed himself in a false position.*

The scene was set. By the end of the year six new adventures had appeared. Sales of the *Strand Magazine* soared, and people queued at bookstalls to buy each new issue. Sherlock Holmes, Dr Watson and Arthur Conan Doyle had become household names, and remain so to this day. He wrote happily and profitably for two years at their new home in South Norwood. His wife, Louise, fell ill however in November 1893. She had tuberculosis. There was no cure, only complete rest and fresh air. There were two children now and the whole family removed to Switzerland, where they took up residence in Davos. Conan Doyle continued to write there very successfully. *The Stark Munro Letters* date from this time and his other 'larger-than-life' character, as Geoffrey Stavert calls him, Brigadier Gerard.

They came home however in 1895 when Conan Doyle was persuaded by a friend living in Hindhead that the air of the South Downs was as beneficial as the air in Davos, and a great deal less expensive. Therefore he set about securing a plot of

The Clarence Memorial and Pier Hotel, *c. 1900. Beyond the* Pier Hotel *is Southsea Terrace where Doyle stayed so curiously in 1896.* PMRS

land in Hindhead and commissioned plans for a house from Portsmouth architect Henry Ball. The scheme fell badly behind schedule, though – Ball was working simultaneously on St Agatha's, Landport for the charismatic Father Dolling. Conan Doyle was therefore forced to rent accommodation nearby in Haslemere for Louise and the children. Thwarted by this temporary setback, it seems that Conan Doyle could not settle to work in Haslemere and he reappears in Southsea. The guest lists published in the local newspapers record on Saturday 16 May 1896 that Dr Conan Doyle has taken up temporary residence at No. 4, Southsea Terrace, a substantial apartment block at the bottom of the Terraces overlooking Southsea Common which is still standing today. He was there for well over six weeks.

Staying nearby at the *Grosvenor Hotel,* where Conan Doyle had been dined out by the Literary and Scientific Society only six years before, were Mrs and Miss Leckie. They were there for the weeks ending 2 May, 9 May and 16 May. We do not know where Conan Doyle met Miss Leckie but for at least ten years between 1896 and 1906 when Louise died, Conan Doyle was self-confessedly in love with Miss Leckie, the daughter of an apparently wealthy Scottish merchant living in Blackheath.

He may indeed have come down to Portsmouth to work, and to look up old friends – and have met Miss Leckie there for the first time entirely fortuitously but equally, he may have come down to rendezvous in Southsea with the young lady. His developing relationship with her may also explain why, shortly before he returned to Haslemere, he purchased 53, Kent Road, known as South View Lodge, for the sum of £1800. Geoffrey Stavert has suggested that Conan Doyle purchased the house to help an old medical friend who was financially embarrassed at this time but it is also possible that he had other plans at this time, for the property, a place perhaps to meet Miss Leckie, whom he married finally in 1907 in the presence of several of his Portsmouth friends including Percy Boulnois.

Writing in his autobiography in 1924, he declared that if he had to live outside London it would be to Southsea that he would return. It is perhaps not surprising. There he began his literary career, met his first wife and may, indeed, have courted the woman who became his second wife.

Selected Bibliography

Allen, Lake, *The History of Portsmouth*, 1817.

Carson, Edward, 'Smugglers and Revenue Officers in the Portsmouth area in the Eighteenth Century', *P(ortsmouth) P(aper)* No. 22, 1974.

Cramer, James, 'History of the Police of Portsmouth', *P.P.* No. 2, 1967, reprinted 1983.

Cramer, James, *Death on the Common at Portsmouth, 1782. An Account of the Trial and Execution of David Tyrie for High Treason*, Portsmouth, 1986.

Cohen, Sheldon S., 'Thomas Wren, Portsmouth's Patron of American Liberty', *P.P.* No. 57, 1991.

Dictionary of National Biography, Online. Specially written biographies of 50,000 men and women who have shaped our past from earliest times to 2000.

Dymond, Dorothy, 'Portsmouth and the fall of the Puritan Republic', *P.P.* No. 11, 1971, reprinted 1979.

Dymond, Dorothy, 'Captain John Mason and the Duke of Buckingham', *P.P.* No. 17, 1972.

East, Robert (Ed.) *Extracts from Records in the Possession of the Municipal Corporation of Portsmouth and from Other Documents relating thereto*, Portsmouth, 1891.

French, Gerald, *The Martyrdom of Admiral Byng*, Glasgow, 1961.

Gates, William G and successors (Eds.), *City of Portsmouth. Records of the Corporation, 1835-1974,* 7 vols. Portsmouth, 1928-83.

Gates, William, *Illustrated History of Portsmouth,* Portsmouth, 1900.

Geddes, Alastair, 'Portsmouth during the Great French Wars, 1770-1800', *P.P.* No. 9, 1970, reprinted 1980.

Hale, Don, *The Last Dive,* 2007.

Harwood, Joy, *Portrait of Portsea 1840-1940,* Portsmouth, 1990.

Hoad, Margaret, 'Portsmouth – As Others have Seen it', (Part 1 1540-1790), *P.P.* No. 15, 1972; (Part 2 1790-1900), *P.P.* No. 20, 1973.

Jordan, Robert, 'Portsmouth in the Glorious Revolution of 1688', *P.P.* No. 54, 1988.

Lilley, Henry T., and Everitt, Alfred T., *Portsmouth Parish Church,* 1921.

Martin, G.H. (Ed.), 'Portsmouth Royal Charters 1194-1974', P(ortsmouth R(ecord) S(eries) Vol. 9, 1995.

Patterson, A. Temple, 'The Naval Mutiny at Spithead, 1797', *P.P.* No. 5, 1968, reprinted 1978.

Pugh, Marshall, *Commander Crabb,* 1956.

Quail, Sarah with Rosalinda Hardiman, *Civic Pride and Sterling Silver. The Civic Plate and Insignia of the City of Portsmouth, 1988.*

Quail, Sarah, Barrett, George, and Chessun, Christopher (Eds.), *Consecrated to Prayer: A Centenary History of St Mary's, Portsea, 1889-1989,* Portsmouth, 1989.

Quail, Sarah, 'The Origins of Portsmouth and the First Charter', *P.P.* 65, 1994.

Quail, Sarah and Wilkinson, Alan (Eds.), *Forever Building. Essays to Mark the Completion of the Cathedral Church of St Thomas of Canterbury Portsmouth,* Portsmouth, 1995.

Quail, Sarah, *Southsea Past,* 2000.

Quail, Sarah, *Portsmouth. A History and Celebration,* 2005.

Riley, R.C., 'The Growth of Southsea as a Naval Satellite and Victorian Resort', *P.P.* No 16, *1972.*

Stanford, Jean and Patterson, A. Temple, 'The Condition of the Children of the Poor in mid-Victorian Portsmouth', *P.P.* No. 21, 1974.

Stavert, Geoffrey, *A Study in Southsea. From Bush Villas to Baker Street,* 1987.

Surry, N.W. and Thomas, J.H. (Eds.), 'Book of Original Entries 1731-1751', *P.R.S.* Vol. 3, 1976.

Thomas, James H., 'Portsmouth and the First Fleet 1786-1787', *P.P.* No. 50, 1987.

Webb, John, 'The Siege of Portsmouth in the Civil War', *P.P.* No. 7, 1968, reprinted with revisions 1977.

Webb, John, 'An Early Victorian Street – the High Street, Old Portsmouth, *P.P.* No. 26, 1977.

Webb, John and others, *Hampshire Studies,* Portsmouth, 1981.

Webb, John, Quail, Sarah, Haskell, Patricia and Riley, Ray, *The Spirit of Portsmouth A History,* 1989.

Willis, Arthur J. and Hoad, Margaret J. (Eds.), 'Borough Sessions Papers 1653-1688', *P.R.S.* Vol. 3, 1971.

The Late Archdeacon Wright, *The Domus Dei or Royal Garrison Church,* Portsmouth, 1873.

Xavier, Sister M. Francis, R.S.M., *A Short Life of Blessed Margaret Pole, Countess. of Salisbury 1473 – 1541,* no date.

York, Neil L., 'Burning the Dockyard. John the Painter and the American Revolution', *P.P.* No. 71, 2001.

TRUE CRIME FROM WHARNCLIFFE
Foul Deeds and Suspicious Deaths Series

Barking, Dagenham & Chadwell Heath
Barnsley
Bath
Bedford
Birmingham
Black Country
Blackburn and Hyndburn
Bolton
Bradford
Brighton
Bristol
Cambridge
Carlisle
Chesterfield
Colchester
Coventry
Croydon
Derby
Dublin
Durham
Ealing
Folkestone and Dover
Grimsby
Guernsey
Guildford
Halifax
Hampstead, Holborn and St Pancras
Huddersfield
Hull

Leeds
Leicester
Lewisham and Deptford
Liverpool
London's East End
London's West End
Manchester
Mansfield
More Foul Deeds Birmingham
More Foul Deeds Chesterfield
More Foul Deeds Wakefield
Newcastle
Newport
Norfolk
Northampton
Nottingham
Oxfordshire
Pontefract and Castleford
Portsmouth
Rotherham
Scunthorpe
Southend-on-Sea
Staffordshire and The Potteries
Stratford and South Warwickshire
Tees
Warwickshire
Wigan
York

OTHER TRUE CRIME BOOKS FROM WHARNCLIFFE

A-Z of Yorkshire Murder
Black Barnsley
Brighton Crime and Vice 1800-2000
Durham Executions
Essex Murders
Executions & Hangings in Newcastle
   and Morpeth
Norfolk Mayhem and Murder

Norwich Murders
Strangeways Hanged
The A-Z of London Murders
Unsolved Murders in Victorian and
   Edwardian London
Unsolved Norfolk Murders
Unsolved Yorkshire Murders
Yorkshire's Murderous Women

Please contact us via any of the methods below for more information or a catalogue.
WHARNCLIFFE BOOKS
47 Church Street – Barnsley – South Yorkshire – S70 2AS
Tel: 01226 734555 – 734222 Fax: 01226 – 734438
E-mail: enquiries@pen-and-sword.co.uk
Website: www.wharncliffebooks.co.uk

Index